Precision Management

Precision Management

How to build
and manage
The
Winning
Organization

By Richard Lynch

Abbott Press
Seattle
1988

Special Thanks to Helen
for her help and encouragement.

Second Printing, May 1988

Abbott Press
732 17th Avenue East
Seattle, WA 98112

Cover designed by Ed Marquand

ISBN 0-933445-00-8

Table of Contents

Chapter 1

What Is
The Winning Organization?

Today, leaders in Western organizations have a great sense that our once-envied management procedures are no longer doing the job. In business, government, and in the nonprofit sector, organizations are withering, becoming less viable, producing fewer results with more people at greater cost. The activity inside the organization may be as furious as ever, but the modern organization is slow to respond to the opportunities of the ever-changing world that surrounds it. As a result, business drowns in the tide of foreign competition, and government and nonprofit organizations find themselves unable to provide needed services in an efficient manner.

As productivity and morale have dwindled among both white- and blue-collar workers, most organizations have responded by treating symptoms, leaving the source of the problem untouched. As a result, errors continue to increase as quality control is added; loyalty continues to decline as wages are raised; grievances continue to multiply as supervisors are trained in communications skills.

Many people now look to Japanese managers for answers. There are a few American organizations, however, that have escaped the progressive ossification of their competitors. These few produce increasingly valuable results in good times and bad. They continue to be viable even as others falter because they are structured and managed in a different way. I call these "Winning Organizations" because in the race to prosper, they quickly outdistance those whose creaking procedures and rigid structures respond too slowly to the promise and the peril in their futures.

Precision Management

A Parable

I like to dramatize the difference between The Winning Organization and its less effective counterparts by telling the following parable. For purposes of this story, I would like you to imagine that I am a typical American white-collar worker. It really doesn't matter what I do specifically, because the problem is the same whether I work for city government, a school district, a large manufacturing corporation, or a nonprofit agency. Each is typically structured and managed by the same assumptions.

In any case, the major and depressing fact about me is that I go to work. I go to work five days a week, and my life between 7:00 A.M. Monday when I get up and 7:00 P.M. Friday when I get home is one vast gray expanse. The dreariness of my hours is unrelieved by my coworkers because their situations are just as dismal as mine. I am dimly aware that I don't get much done, but as I sit here forcing my way through this routine, mind-rotting task, I figure they're lucky to get anything out of me at all.

At other times, I think something must be wrong with me. After all, why shouldn't I be satisfied with this job? I make good money. Each year I get a raise, just for sticking it out. The benefit plan is the best in town. I have a closet full of the latest fashions, a new car, a Presto Hot-dogger—all the good things in life. Why shouldn't I be happy?

I am not alone in being baffled by this. Management is constantly asking us workers what's wrong, through various attitude surveys and so forth. And sure enough, a lot of changes have been made. We complained, for example, about the impersonal way the organization treated us, that management regarded us as mere cogs in a machine, and now we all have our nicknames on our desks.

We complained about the depressing atmosphere, and they had the walls painted yellow.

We complained that there was no sense of team spirit, that there were too many conflicts within the organization, and now we are in a bowling league. And in the summer, we play golf together.

We complained that we didn't seem to be appreciated, and now we have an employee appreciation banquet every year.

We complained about the low status of the organization in the community, that no one wanted to admit he worked here, and now we have the most generous package of fringe benefits of any place in town. We have a great retirement plan, and we have more sick leave and vacation time than anyone else. They also raised our salary scale.

We complained that our supervisor treated us unfairly, and they packed her off to California for sensitivity training. Whereas she used to say things like "You hopeless idiot, you can't do anything right," now she says "What I hear you saying is that your head is in a different space."

We complained there was no sense of accomplishment, and now they give us plaques for our walls each year, thanking us for our contributions.

But while all these changes were nice, they didn't change the way I felt about my job. I still hated it. In fact, the only thing I responded to very much in all of those changes was the weekend golf games. I must say, I really looked forward to those. In fact, I spent most of my time at work in the summer mentally replaying last weekend's round and daydreaming about next weekend's. I liked playing golf so much that I got up at 5:30 in the morning and drove 32 miles and stood in line for four hours to get to do it.

But, if anything, this only made my job seem more dismal by comparison. The rest of the year, I sat, like my coworkers, counting the hours until quitting time, the days until the next vacation, the years till retirement. And this scared me because it meant we were all trying to get our lives over with as quickly as possible.

That was my situation until one Friday afternoon, deep in the depression of my demeaning, paper-shuffling job, working at a snail's pace because concentrating on this stuff too long causes you to go mad, I shouted "I hate this!" Fortunately, it was 6:00 and there was nobody else around.

And that felt kind of good, blurting that out after all those years of frustration, and so I went on shouting. "I hate this job. Why does my job have to be so boring? Why can't it be fun and exciting? Like ... like playing golf. If I could get as much satisfaction out of my job as I do out of playing golf, I'd ... sell my soul to the Devil!"

To my astonishment, there was a puff of smoke, and a little red man with horns appeared and said, "Sold!"

Needless to say, I was terrified. But as the Devil walked off with my soul, chuckling to himself, I began to wonder. And the more I wondered, the more excited I became. What if my job, the bulk of my waking hours, were as satisfying and rewarding as a game of golf. Of course, there was the little matter of eternal damnation to consider, but still, what a life that would be. I started wishing that tomorrow were a workday, because I could hardly wait to see how the Devil was going to pull this off.

But the next day was Saturday, and so I found myself out at the golf course as usual. As I was loosening up on the first tee, however, the club pro stopped me and said there were going to be some changes in the way we played from now on. He explained that while the balls would still go around the course as usual, we would all be spared the silly effort of chasing after them and would concentrate instead on a particular shot that we did well. My role, chosen after a thorough analysis of my abilities and attributes, was to make the first putt on the sixth green.

He took my clubs and handed me a putter. "Hey," I said, "why can't I use my own putter? I'd never buy a putter like this; it's too short."

"Now, now," he said, "we can't have everyone doing things his own way. That would cause massive inefficiencies for the purchasing department. Besides, we've conducted an exhaustive survey of putters and found that this is the best one for the job. Not to mention its being made by the low bidder."

He took me out to the sixth hole and introduced me to the sixth-hole supervisor, who was a really good golfer. In fact, as I looked around the course, it seemed all the best golfers had been made supervisors.

Pretty soon, the first ball made its way to the sixth hole, and it was time for my first putt. Now, the turkey whose job it was to hit the ball onto the green had left me about a hundred feet from the hole. I got down, lined it up, and I made one of the most brilliant putts in the history of golf. The ball went up a hill, down a hill, broke three different ways, and slid just past the hole, stopping about a foot away. Boy, they sure picked the right guy for this job, I said to myself.

But the idiot who was in charge of making the second putt miraculously missed it. "Hey, come on," my supervisor said. "Let's go, team. We can do better than that."

"It's not my fault," said the guy who missed the putt. "Lynch left me with a tricky little downhill, side-hill putt."

"Heck, it was only a foot long," I said. "Besides, that jerk who hit the ball on the green left me six miles from the hole. I couldn't even see it from where I was."

"It's not my fault," the guy in the fairway yelled. "That woman with the driver hit the ball into a hole out here. I was lucky to get it on the green at all."

"Well, it was right in the middle of the fairway," she yelled, and pretty soon we were all standing around squabbling.

Finally, the front-nine supervisor came over to intervene. She pulled my supervisor aside and said, "You can't let things get out of control like this. Give them some guidance. Show some leadership."

Sure enough, when I got ready to make my next putt, my boss was breathing over my shoulder telling me how much break to allow and how hard to hit it.

Now this next putt was a tricky 20-footer with the same double break as my previous one. My supervisor didn't see this, but that was okay because I knew it was there. So I ignored his advice and hit it directly into the center of the hole. I turned around to receive my congratulations. I looked to my supervisor, but he was busy being congratulated by his boss. I turned to the second putter; he looked depressed. I looked out to the fairway to the guy who hit the ball on the green. He said "Hey, come on, get off the green, I've got three more out here."

As the morning wore on, I continued to make some pretty good puts, despite my supervisor's help. But after a while, it started to make less and less difference to me. My mind started to wander, even as I was preparing for the shot. I started to look forward to having a cold drink.

"Hey," I said. "Don't we ever get a break?"

"Yeah, Lynch is right," said the second putter. "It's hot out here."

"We've got more balls to play," my supervisor said.

"I don't care," I said. "I want a break."

"Just hit the ball," he said.

The front-nine supervisor came over and whispered to him. "We've got to watch that Lynch. He's a troublemaker."

"I heard that," I yelled, "and if you think you've got trouble now, wait till you see what happens if I don't get a break."

To my surprise a cheer went up all over the course, and people started chanting "We want a break! We want a break!" It was fantastic.

The supervisors looked around and quickly caved in. My fellow golfers carried me to the clubhouse on their shoulders, and we celebrated with a beer. It was a lot of fun. But unfortunately, pretty soon the break was over, and we had to go back out to play golf.

When we did, my boss went on lining up my putts, and as he did so, he started getting on my nerves. After a while, though, he saw that the guy in the fairway really was hopeless and went out to give him some pointers. When he came back, he found balls all over the green.

"I was waiting for you to tell me what to do," I explained. His exasperation was oddly satisfying.

He got down and lined up the next one. My heart soared with the thrill of victory for the first time that day as I hit it exactly as he told me and the putt stopped ten feet from the hole.

About that time, the iron player cut a ball. Our boss submitted a request to purchasing for a new one. They sent it back, saying it wasn't filled out right and asking for an evaluation of the reason for this mishap and a plan for reducing cut balls. So we had a meeting about this, which I was forced to attend even though I wasn't about to cut a ball with my putter. All over the course, I noticed, similar meetings were being held, bogging things down.

Shortly after we started playing again, at about two o'clock, the driver, who had been uniformly hitting the ball into the dead center of the fairway, screamed "I hate this!" and quit.

As the balls from the fifth hole piled up on the tee, we had to wait in the blistering sun while they interviewed people for her position. Finally, I said to the supervisor, "Look, the whole course is getting held up here. I wouldn't mind hitting drives for a while."

The supervisor smiled. "Sally's a hard person to replace," he said with overwhelming warmth. "Besides, we need you for putting."

"No you don't. Without a driver, there are no balls to putt," I fumed.

He patted me on the shoulder. "Let me think it over. Meanwhile, since you have nothing to do, it would be useful if you would go over the green on your hands and knees and smooth out any little bumps you find and pick up any grains of sand or twigs so we can make sure we have a true surface to putt on."

"That's ridiculous," I said.

"No, it's not. What if, on your next putt, the ball hits a little rock or an indentation and gets knocked off line. Wouldn't it have been useful for you to have used this spare time now to head that off?"

Well, finally, 176 grains of sand later, we got going again. As we did, I noticed that although the new driver was about as good as Sally, our scores continued to deteriorate. As they got worse, our supervisor began to rant and rave at us. I recall one occasion with particular vividness. The ball was just off the green and the boss said "Come on, Lynch, what are you waiting for? Hit the ball."

I said "That ball is not yet on the green. It is not in my job description to hit a ball that is not on the green."

"It's close enough," he said. "Now get over there and do it."

"I don't have the tools to hit a ball that is not on the green. It's buried in the grass, and I can't tell how fast it will come out. Now if I had a six-iron, I could chip it . . . "

"If you had a six-iron, I would bend it over your head. Now hit the ball!"

So I hit it. The ball skipped clear across the green and into a sand trap. My boss ranted and steamed and turned red as a beet, but I didn't much care. I was getting bored, and his carrying on was the only excitement we got.

Along about Sunday afternoon, I found I was just hitting the ball and not even looking to see where it went. During the final hour on Sunday, our lowest score on the sixth hole was a 12. I was shocked to hear my supervisor mutter under his breath, "I hate this," because I was just thinking the same thing myself. I went away from the course that night feeling the same about my favorite game as I did about work.

The Devil, of course, was to blame for this, arranging it so I'd get the same satisfaction from golf as from work. But, I thought, maybe, by implication, he had also shown me a way out my dilemma. After all, if he could make my favorite game as boring as work, could we do the opposite at work to make our jobs as satisfying as my favorite game?

The Devil's Lesson

When I tell this story in my management seminars, I then ask "What's wrong with playing golf this way?" Participants typically give answers such as "no creativity," "lack of responsibility for an end product," "no respect for me as a whole person," "no control over what I do." These answers, of course, are the same ones we hear when we ask people today "What's wrong with your job?"

The main point of the story, then, is that it is possible to organize any activity so it is boring and demeaning and destructive to the motivation of the individual. The way to do this is to organize it the way work is typically organized. And while it may seem absurd to organize golf in this way, it would seem just as absurd to us to organize work in this way if it weren't the norm to do so.

In my seminars I also ask, "If the golf course management called you in as a consultant to suggest ways to combat low morale, dwindling productivity, and high turnover, what solution would you recommend?" The answers I get to this question tend to be the same answers that consultants frequently give managers of troubled organizations: "establish quality circles on each hole to discuss ways to improve"; "let us rotate jobs"; "send our supervisor to training"; "give us incentive bonuses"; "encourage me to try out new ways of putting"; "give us longer lunch hours"; "establish performance standards"; "institute a tough quality control program;" "send us to hear a motivational speaker." It is rare that someone has the audacity to suggest that each player play all 18 holes, although occasionally someone will suggest letting each golfer hit all the shots on one hole. Perhaps people rarely suggest letting players play the whole course because it is such a radical departure from the way things are being done. But it is the only solution that will solve the problem because the problem is structural; the various symptoms that people identify as being "wrong" all stem from the way the work is defined and organized.

We have, in short, designed jobs in our society in a way that insures that our people will avoid responsibility, take no initiative, work as slowly as possible, demonstrate little intelligence, avoid making decisions, and show little concern for the needs or goals of the organization. Faced with people who behave in this way, managers make matters worse by responding with authoritarian methods of supervision that demean the worker and produce resentment, alienation, and apathy. In such a context, none of the traditional incentives will buy our loyalty, because when work is deprived of its meaning, the only sense of achievement we can get in the workplace is to succeed in thwarting the organization. All the motivational speakers in the world won't turn us into "winners" because when we get to the job, there is nothing to win.

In contrast, managers in The Winning Organization design work that is challenging, rewarding, and interesting for each employee. Workers in The Winning Organization are therefore disposed to take responsibility, seek out opportunities, work hard toward the achievement of organizational goals, and grow in their abilities. Once these hospitable conditions are established, managers in The Winning Organization supervise their people in ways which produce commitment in place of apathy, pride in place of alienation, and loyalty in place of hostility.

Precision Management Advantages

The differences between the Precision Management approach taken by these effective organizations and their less productive counterparts is summarized below. Each of these points is expanded in the remainder of the book.

Precision Management is more efficient and creates better morale in part because it places responsibility at the lowest level. Standard management fragments responsibility, with many workers and often many divisions having a hand in the final product. The result of this fragmentation is that only top management is responsible for the final product.

Because of this fragmentation, standard management creates inevitable turf battles, with frustrated workers vying for more authority over the final product.

Precision Management makes workers responsible for a whole product. They go to work to produce something and hence are more likely to do so than workers in traditional organizations who are responsible only for performing a certain number of activities or for working a certain number of hours.

Precision Management enables the worker and the supervisor to tell at all times if the worker is succeeding in accomplishing the results for which he is responsible. In traditionally managed organizations, workers have no sense of whether they are winning or losing. The terms mean nothing to them, with the consequence that their enthusiasm and commitment suffer.

Precision Management regards a worker's failure to produce his results as a reflection of his competence. Unlike traditional managers, however, a manager using Precision Management methods treats failure as a sign that the worker needs to grow, not that he needs to be punished. She sits down with the worker to examine the reasons for failure, to help him learn from his experience, and to help him establish a plan, which is his responsibility to carry out, to improve. The manager's role is to help each worker succeed in his effort to achieve the results that are his responsibility.

Organizations structured on Precision Management principles are leaner than traditional organizations. They require less staff and less management to produce results than traditional organizations.

Long chains of command in traditional organizations are fine for translating orders, procedures, and policies from the top but do not work well when people at the bottom have an idea and must send it up the chain for approval. Since workers are the leading experts on the current state of what is happening in their jobs, they are the only ones, sometimes, who are in a position to know that something is wrong (that a manual they use is out of date, for example), yet they feel powerless to make a change. Recommendations going up the chain require so many people to approve them before any action can be taken, that workers often feel it is pointless even to try. If they do try, the time it takes for action is so long, that they frequently feel the recommendation has vanished into a void. Precision Management encourages a results-oriented structure that enables workers to make many decisions without approval or managers close to the worker to approve recommendations. The Winning Organization is thus quicker to react and to improve the way the work is done.

The Precision Management approach enables each employee to get the most impact possible from each hour of his day. Standard management pays a premium for vast amounts of work time that is used for socializing or eaten up in trivia.

Precision Management offers supervisors a way to empower workers to achieve results without giving up control themselves. Traditional managers, in trying to control things, belittle and diminish the workers. It is easier to get results from empowered people than from belittled people.

When corrective action needs to be taken, supervisors using Precision Management methods do so in a way that builds worker self-esteem, while traditional supervisors do so in ways that are destructive to the individual.

Precision Management enables the manager to tap the four most powerful motivational needs of modern workers: the need for achievement, the need for control, the need for growth, and the need for recognition. Traditional management does too little in each of these areas, with the result that workers have negative attitudes toward their work and their employer.

The culture produced by Precision Management methods imbues in its members a sense of strength, importance, and effectiveness that drives them toward excellence in their work life. Traditional organizations' cultures tend to work against such feelings.

Precision Management also leads to a more natural and successful method of strategic planning. While traditional organizations suffer because their planning methods are too tedious or too out-of-touch or too late to make a difference, managers in The Winning Organization, with their outward, results-oriented frame of reference, naturally make plans that lead to greater success. While traditional organizations are continually responding to the problems and surprises the future brings them, managers in The Winning Organization, through their more effective planning, create a future in which they can succeed.

In sum, the advantages of The Winning Organization are that its workers are more motivated, its methods of operation are more efficient, and its overhead is lower. It moves faster, more surely, and produces results of a higher quality than its counterparts. It is less riven with factions and has more unity of purpose than other organizations.

In the following chapters, we will explore how The Winning Organization makes maximum use of the talents of its people. The approaches spelled out in these chapters have been tested in a variety of businesses, government agencies, and nonprofit organizations. They have improved the productivity and morale in small organizations with only one manager as well as in large, multi-divisional operations. The next four chapters tell how such organizations have altered the way they define work in order to motivate people to top performance. The last five chapters tell how best to manage people within the winning structure once you have created it.

Chapter 2

Designing Jobs for Results

An organization's effectiveness depends on the ability of its workers to produce results. One of the most obvious things a manager can do to ensure that her people produce results is to give them clear responsibility for achieving clearly defined results. Yet the vast majority of workers today are like the golfers in chapter one; they are responsible only for a process—for performing an activity—not a whole product.

In order for workers to be responsible, hard-working, and enthusiastic, their jobs must have three characteristics: The employees must have a sense of ownership of the job, or "turf"; they must know clearly what results they are supposed to achieve; and they must have the opportunity to do the thinking necessary to achieve those results. While designing jobs in this way is harder in some instances than in others, it is always possible for any job worth paying for. Unless you are operating your organization as a welfare program for workers, you can't afford to hire people for jobs in which these three things can't be defined.

Giving Workers Turf

The first step in developing a work structure that encourages excellence is to make sure each worker has "turf." By having turf, I mean that the employee has something of his own to be responsible for—his own clients, his own geographical area, his own products. This "ownership" implies that the worker (or, in some cases, teams of workers as we will see later) controls all that happens on his turf, that he alone is responsible for the success or failure of the activities conducted with relation to that turf. For example, a park maintenance worker might be responsible for the activities connected with maintaining a given park instead of doing one activity (such as picking up the trash) in all the parks. A police officer might be responsible for investigating a case from the time of the first call until the final disposition instead of doing one activity (such as securing the crime scene or contacting witnesses). Or a telephone book compiler might be responsible for all the activities necessary to produce one book instead of doing one activity (such as alphabetizing the white pages) on many books. When jobs are transformed in this way, workers report an increase in pride in their work and in job satisfaction, and management finds that errors, absenteeism, turnover, and grievances decline dramatically.

Yet this way of organizing work is in direct contradiction to the way work is normally organized. Work is not normally defined in this way because, on paper, it seems that the standard approach would be more efficient. It seems efficient to have each person do a small part of the whole because a single task can be mastered quickly. Because only one skill is called for, and because that skill will be used repeatedly, it seems reasonable that this approach to job design would give us the best chance of the work being done without any mistakes. If the worker does not do defect-free work, the standard approach is to make the job simpler, to make it smaller—"so easy a monkey can do it"—so that he can do it without a mistake. Managers who take this reasonable approach are typically puzzled by the fact that errors often increase when jobs are made simpler. They also fail to connect the rise in work-stoppages, grievances, and outright worker sabotage to this way of organizing work.

While the traditional approach may once have worked better than it does now, today's managers will always suffer from under-motivated workers when work is fragmented in the standard way. Today's workers simply do not look forward to spending a whole day doing a job that a monkey could do. They do it, but they do it because they have to make a living. Their work life is thus an unpleasant necessity, a drab expanse between weekends. They invest little thought or creative energy in their work because such is not called for. They therefore contribute only a fraction of their true potential and worth to the organization.

Effective organizations find it easier to get results, in part, because their workers want to do the work. They look forward to work each day because it satisfies them as much as other workers' leisure activities do. And such workers will always produce better results than those who "have" to work.

Here are two examples, from different settings, of how motivation increases and management becomes easier and more effective when the worker is given some turf.

The first example comes from a state welfare office. The office employed 66 workers in its financial section. These workers were divided into three units. The job of the first unit was taking applications for financial assistance. A second unit was in charge of investigating whether the applicant was eligible for assistance. And the third unit was responsible for maintenance—for making sure people who were approved received their checks or other assistance. Maintenance was divided into four sub-units, each in charge of a certain number of cases and each with its own supervisor. These four supervisors were paid less than the supervisors of other sub-units, and maintenance workers were paid less than the other financial workers.

This system appeared efficient on the surface. The intake worker took the application, passed it on to investigation for approval, and the approved application went to maintenance for action.

In reality, however, the system was fraught with delay and frustration, and clients were inefficiently served. The system was made more complicated by the fact that in some cases, where the client was to be given assistance on the basis of his incapacity, the assistance had to be approved by an incapacity specialist who worked in a different section of the office.

Further, hidden, inefficiencies resulted from the handling of the application. In each step of the process, the worker who received the paper had to mentally redo the work of the previous worker. A worker in the investigations unit, for example, had to go through the application before he could proceed with the investigation in order to understand what the intake worker already knew. Sometimes he might see what appeared to be an error or omission in the application and would send it back to the intake unit. Once it got there, it was routed to an intake worker, not always the one who completed the original application. This person found out why the application appeared to be incorrect or incomplete, often discovering there was a good reason for it. The explanation was then pinned to the application and sent back to investigation where usually a different investigator reviewed the application to learn what now three other people already knew. Similarly, the maintenance workers had to review the work of the previous two units.

At supervisory meetings, free-for-all arguments frequently took place. The supervisor of the clerical section, for example, might report that the receptionist had just received a desperate phone call from someone who had applied for assistance weeks ago and had not yet received a determination of eligibility. The manager of the financial section would demand to know the facts. The supervisors would find out the facts and then begin to blame each other. "I can't issue a check until an investigation is complete." "I can't make a determination on this case because it is an incapacity question, and I'm not the incapacity supervisor." And so on.

In addition to complaints from clients, the office suffered from a very high turnover rate among financial section workers, particularly those in maintenance. Grievances from employees were frequently filed, and absenteeism was also a problem.

If you were a consultant and were called in to deal with the low morale, dwindling productivity, and client complaints that plagued this office, what solution would you recommend? (It is the same solution that applied in the golf situation in the previous chapter.) Think about your answer before you read on.

If you answered "give each financial worker responsibility for a given group of clients for which they did all three tasks" your answer would indeed give each worker turf, thereby forming the basis for a satisfying and effective job.

When I suggested this solution to the supervisors of this office, the response was "But that's the way we used to do it 16 years ago." As I asked them to describe how things had been back then, they described high work satisfaction and greater service to clients. Over the years, the system had been made more "sophisticated," more "scientific," more complicated, and as a result the workers were robbed of the essential satisfaction of helping people in distress. More supervisors were added to deal with the problems produced by this new way of organizing things, and the cost of serving people rose. By having given people their natural "turf," in this case a set of clients, the office had previously worked more efficiently.

Let's take a more complicated example next. Most of us are passingly familiar with the job of the bank teller, though most of us don't realize the motivational toll such a position can take on the worker. People in this job are usually low paid and the opportunities for advancement are limited. There is a certain a-mount of stress related to making sure the till balances at the end of the day, but it is not the sort of stress that pushes the worker to higher achievement. If mistakes are made, the teller is usually punished (pay docked or the teller suspended), but if the job is done well, there are few, if any, rewards.

One bank saw an opportunity to make the teller's job more interesting—and at the same time increase its profits—when the federal government began to deregulate the banking industry. Banks were plunged into a fiercely competitive environment where savings and loan institutions, credit unions, and stock brokers began to offer services previously provided only by banks. At the same time, banks were able to offer customers many new types of accounts; while this was an opportunity for the banks, customers were often confused by the profusion of services they could now get from their bank.

In response to this, the bank decided it either needed to hire new people or make better use of the ones it already had. Management saw tellers as one group that was underutilized. Following Precision Management job design principles, management gave tellers their own turf by dividing current customers among the tellers. A sales consultant trained the tellers in sales techniques, and they were given a certain period of time each day to make calls to their customers to sell bank services. For each new service sold, the teller received a bonus (for example, 100 dollars for an individual retirement account).

As you might expect, tellers began putting out extra effort. Some called on "their customers" on their own time, making face-to-face presentations. Gradually, tellers developed personal relationships with many bank customers, creating increased customer loyalty to the bank. And the bank's profits increased, even while those of their larger competitors declined. (It is significant that this was a relatively small bank: larger institutions are generally so fragmented in their structure that committees would have to be formed to even consider such an approach, at which point it would probably be studied to death. We will return to that problem in chapter four.)

Managers often resist the idea of giving a worker his own turf. Perhaps they resist because it is such a radical change; most would like to get better results without doing anything very different. In response to the stress they feel when faced with such changes, many managers grope for excuses as to why they can't do this ("the union wouldn't stand for it" or "my boss wouldn't go for this"). But for those who find the initial strength to act, to give their workers "turf," life becomes far less stressful. It is much easier to succeed in any endeavor when people you lead share a sense of ownership and pride in the enterprise. This is accomplished by giving workers turf and is one way in which results-oriented managers build The Winning Organization.

The Responsibility for Thinking

The second key element in designing jobs for results is to make sure that employees have the authority to think as well as "do" the job. By thinking, I mean the planning, organizing, deciding, and evaluating of what the worker does on his turf.

Again, many managers have a built-in resistance to turning over these functions to employees because they have been taught that these are management responsibilities. They believe that it is the supervisor's job personally to control, plan, and evaluate what her people do.

The problems this belief has caused for our society, our organizations, and the mental health of our managers and workers would take another book to recount. For our purposes, however, the chief problem with this practice is that it separates two types of functions that are more efficient when done by one person—thinking and doing.

Standard management practice holds that it is the manager's job to do the thinking and the employee's job to do whatever "doing" the thinker decides needs to be done. It assumes that this is a good idea because the manager is smarter than the worker. If you have your smartest people do the thinking—the planning, organizing, and evaluating—and others doing these smart things, it seems, on paper, that this should get you the best results.

Under this theory, any doers who become outstanding at doing what the thinker decides get promoted to be thinkers. Which means, in order to get to be a thinker, you have to prove yourself as a non-thinker. As a result, many struggling organizations have a lot of outstanding non-thinkers in management positions.

By contrast, Precision Management systems allow the worker to control as many factors related to producing the required results as possible. When we allow the worker to think and then perform, we create greater efficiency on two counts: first, we overcome the communications problems that are inevitable when the brain that decides what to do is not directly connected by neural pathways to the body that does the work; and second, we avoid the resentment people feel when they are treated as if they were incapable of thinking things out for themselves (a factor we will return to in chapter six).

Let's explore, then, how we can build this worker responsibility into traditionally "unthinking" jobs. Imagine that you own an independent supermarket. Of all the jobs in your store the clerks' is the least rewarding. Their duties include bagging groceries, stamping prices, stocking shelves, sweeping floors, and unloading trucks. Clerks do all of these things when you decide they should be done and tell them to do so. Because the job contains a variety of tasks, it is not as dull as many other "non-thinking" jobs. It fails to meet the criteria we are exploring in this chapter, however, in that there is no turf, no clear result to try to achieve, and there is no thinking required. In any case, the clerks show little enthusiasm, and there are problems with compliance and turnover. You detect a certain hostility among many of them, and there is talk about joining the retail clerks' union.

Other problems you face include the number of hours you spend in managing the people who work for you and making the necessary administrative decisions so that they will know what to do. In addition to the constant need to hire and train new people, you also work long into the night figuring out work schedules for them. These tasks, in addition to your other duties of checking inventories, ordering, deciding on pricing, figuring out how the merchandise should be displayed, deciding what ads to run, often cause you to work 16 hour days, which is destroying your health, your family life, and your leisure pursuits. In the past two years, you have hired a full-time accountant to look after the financial side of things, and this has helped a little. You have recently given some thought to creating the post of store manager to handle some of your work. But you haven't had time to decide whether to promote one of your three department heads (meat, produce, bakery) or hire someone from the outside. This position would also cut substantially into your profits.

The key to solving the problems you face is to heal the division between thinking and doing in the clerk's job. Before you read on, take a piece of paper and roughly describe what the new job would look like. If you do this right, you will create a job which is more interesting and which motivates them to top performance. What tasks would the new job description contain?

When confronted by the situation described above, most managers attempt to treat the symptoms. For example, they may go to time-management seminars and learn how to prioritize their tasks, how to delegate, and how to work more efficiently. Since the problem is one which affects them, they look to themselves for a solution. The last place they would look is to the job description of their lowest-paid worker, yet it is there that the solution to the problem lies. For in making the job of the clerk whole, we also will greatly reduce the number of hours the retailer need work, and we will increase the store's profitability.

To redesign such an unthinking job, we need to ask what the clerks are told to do by someone else. Once we have identified those tasks (they are essentially the duties mentioned earlier), we ask "What does the boss do in order to figure out what to tell the clerks?" We then transfer this mental responsibility to the clerks, healing the unnatural schism between thinking and doing. In a sense, we give them back their brains.

Before we do that, however, we can build on the lessons of the earlier section of this chapter and give the clerk some turf. In this case, that turf for each is an aisle in the store for which he or she is responsible (in addition to still having some storewide responsibilities). Once we have gotten that far, we can build a job which includes the tasks each is now told to do and which includes the thinking tasks necessary to decide to do those things. A finished job description might be expanded as follows:

ORIGINAL TASKS:
   Prices will be stamped and updated as necessary
   Shelves will be fully stocked to meet demand
   Stockrooms will be clean
   Shelves will be clean
   Groceries for customers will be bagged
   Groceries for customers will be carried out

NEW TASKS: (for the clerk's aisle)
   Shelves will be laid out to give each product
     space relative to demand
   Merchandise will be displayed attractively
   Shelves will be restocked as needed
   Work hours and schedules for cleaning and other
     common tasks will be determined in concert
     with other clerks
   New products to meet consumer needs will be
     identified and purchased
   Sufficient inventory of products will be on hand

One of the reactions I sometimes get from clients on this is "But we'd have to hire different people to do these things. You don't know how stupid, irresponsible, and resistant my people are." And indeed, in this example, such responsibilities may be a big jump for our clerks to make all at once.

But we need not have them make this jump all at once. We can wean them to the new job by first giving them responsibility for stocking shelves on their aisles when necessary. (In the past, the store owner was the one who took all responsibility for seeing if this activity needed to be done.) From there, it is a natural step to give them responsibility for maintaining inventory of the products on their aisles. Then, once they've mastered that, we can give them responsibility for ordering, then determining shelf display, and so on. In this way, we keep them constantly growing; they always have the challenge of a new responsibility to master. This sense of growth is itself a powerful motivator.

Further, the job as previously designed leads people to stupid, irresponsible, and resistant behavior. When, as in traditional organizations, the job is designed so the manager does all the thinking, the manager takes responsibility for the quality of the work. We therefore have the disastrous situation in which the people who do the work are not responsible for its quality, and the people who do not do the work, the supervisors, are. That so many traditional organizations have problems with the quality of their workers' performance is no surprise, given this way of organizing the work. We should never be surprised when people act irresponsibly if they have no real responsibility. When we design the job so that it demands responsibility and commitment, however, it will bring out the best, rather than the worst in people.

Responsibility for Results

The third critical element in developing a work structure that encourages excellence is to make sure that workers are held responsible for achieving results rather than performing a set of activities or "job duties." When we do this, we not only make the job more challenging but make the organization more competitive, more viable. Imagine the increase in effectiveness if school teachers, for example, were paid based on whether their students learned anything instead of on their longevity in the job, if police were responsible for reducing burglaries instead of patrolling the streets, if anti-poverty programs were focussed on getting people out of poverty instead of providing services to the poor. Japanese car manufacturers have dealt a severe blow to the American auto industry in part because their workers are responsible for a result—the quality of the product—instead of the number of operations per hour they perform.

This distinction between holding people responsible for results instead of for activities is so important, with such far-reaching implications, that I want to pause here to make sure the difference is clear. On the next page, in the box, are ten statements taken from job descriptions of people I have worked with in the past. The job title is in parentheses. For each, decide whether it makes the worker responsible for a result—an achievement, an accomplishment, an end product—or if it merely holds him responsible for performing an activity. After you complete the exercise, compare your conclusions with the answers below.

1. This is a clear statement of the result expected from the salesperson's various activities. Increased sales is what we want to hold him or her accountable for, not numbers of calls on customers, hours of meeting with prospects, money spent on advertising, or any of the numerous other activities he or she might engage in to achieve this result. Anyone can call on a customer or spend time with someone—these things take no skill at all. The only meaningful measure of performance is whether the result was achieved.

2. This is merely an activity for the fire marshal to perform. It is a job, once again, that anyone can do. Why do we want the buildings inspected? To reduce the chance that they will catch fire? Then hold the person responsible for reducing the number of fires. Or the amount of fire loss. Or whatever else we want to achieve with the activity of inspecting. This provides the fire marshal with a challenge. And once again, we can measure performance easily.

---

1. (Salesperson) Increase profits from sales by 10 percent this year.

2. (Fire Marshal) Inspect all commercial properties for fire hazards once each year.

3. (Receptionist) People coming to or calling the office will view us as a competent, professional organization.

4. (Trainer) Conduct 15 training sessions per month.

5. (Hospital Food Service Worker) Patients will find their meals appetizing.

6. (Supervisor) Staff will each have the skills necessary to produce the results for which each is responsible.

7. (Teacher) Meet with parents once per quarter.

8. (Clerk) Reduce staff work load through improved office procedures.

9. (Maid) Clients will be satisfied with the tidiness and cleanliness of their homes.

10. (Plant Manager) Analyze and report quarterly to the vice president for operations on plans to improve production.

---

3. This is a good statement of a result of the receptionist's job. Interestingly enough, once the company that hired this particular receptionist realized that this indeed was what they wanted her for, they made her part of the public relations department and increased her salary.

4. Again, this is merely an activity for the trainer to get through; anyone can do this. Why do we want training? To increase the skills of our people? Then make the trainer responsible for that.

5. This is a good—and very challenging—statement of a result for the food service worker to achieve. Although we wouldn't expect anything like 100 percent perfect performance from such workers (they are constrained by the nutritionist in what they can prepare,

and their "customers" are sick) it is still what they should be trying to achieve every time they prepare a meal. This example comes from a hospital that was in a life or death struggle with the other hospital in town. Once this result was placed in the food service worker's job, the tide began to turn in this hospital's favor.

6. Making sure his people have the skills they need to achieve their results is the end-product of activities of coaching, training, and counseling the supervisor engages in. If the supervisor achieves this, his people will be able to produce their results, and that is what we pay him for (in part).

7. This is another activity with no defined point. Anyone can yawn his way through such meetings with parents, and the people holding the teacher responsible for this shouldn't be surprised if these meetings produce no result (none is specified) and if the teachers resent having to stay at school until early evening to meet with working parents.

8. Reducing the workload is a clear result for the person to try to achieve. "Through improved office procedures" confines the person to a certain set of activities in order to achieve the result.

9. This is a result. Some may be tempted to say that a clean house is the result of the maid's activities, but when the house-cleaning firm I worked with on this tried that definition, the problem was deciding what "clean" means. They finally decided that it was the customer's standard that mattered, and so they used customer satisfaction (measured by asking customers if they were satisfied) as the end product of the cleaning activities.

10. If this is indeed what you want the plant manager to be responsible for, you can save a lot of money in administrative overhead by hiring a bright high school student to do this. What is the result of all this analyzing and reporting? That the vice president will know what is going on? Why do we care about that? So we will make sure we improve production? Why not simply make the plant manager responsible for that? When I tried this solution on the client in question, the vice president maintained that improving production was his responsibility. He was the one who dreamed up the plan, and he wanted someone to tell him how well it was going so he could modify the plan if necessary. But in

setting things up in this way, we place the responsibility for the result higher than it need be and at a level where the person responsible is too far removed from the action to move swiftly to improve things. By fixing responsibility in the plant manager ("Improve output per man-hour" being the result) we make his job more interesting and relieve the vice president of the burden so that he can spend his time on tasks more suitable to his station.

This last situation is an example of a common problem ineffective organizations have; they tend to place responsibility for a result several levels higher in the bureaucratic superstructure than is necessary. This not only creates a greater overhead burden (in the 1970s, for example, Ford Motor Company paid for three times the number of levels of management than the much leaner and more effective Toyota), but it also increases the need for communication among the various units. Frequently, additional staff are hired to cope with all of this communication, which only produces more communication, more paper, more files, more "administrivia," and more work for each person. If we can place responsibility for a result in the person who is engaged in producing it, we will not only increase the worker's motivation but weed out unnecessary functions as well.

Types of Responsibility

So far, the examples we have discussed all stress giving a person total, individual responsibility for an end product. In some situations, however, this is not possible nor desirable. For example, the number of skills and body of knowledge required to build a Chevrolet would make the training process very lengthy and costly if we were to have one person perform all the activities necessary to build a whole car. In some cases, in fact, it is physically impossible for one person to do a task. Where a variety of skills must be brought together to do a job, or where there is natural, shared responsibility, a second type of responsibility is required—team responsibility for a result.

Many organizations use the word "team" to describe collections of workers that are not really teams at all. The golfers in chapter one, for example, might have been called a team by their supervisor ("this is my team" and "come on, team" and "let's be the best team on this course"), but they were not really a team because they never had to work together to achieve a result. In reality they had neither individual nor team responsibility for a result, but a third kind of responsibility: they each had partial responsibility for the total result (the score on the sixth hole being a part of the unseen whole). They didn't do the things a team would do; they didn't confer about the shots to be made; they didn't plan strategy; they didn't work together as a cohesive, thinking whole. And the supervisor's efforts to do the thinking and coordinating do not make them a team; in fact, those efforts denied them the activities (the thinking tasks) that would allow them to become one.

An example of team responsibility can be found in the grocery clerks' revised job description. When they work together to set work hours and schedules for bagging, cleaning, and other common tasks, they are carrying out team responsibility for a result. In fact, a great deal of team responsibility is possible. One way of writing such a job description for these people in results-based terms is as follows:

> Individual results:
>   -Sales on clerk's aisle will increase
>   -Customers needs for products will be met
> Team results:
>   -The store will meet health standards
>   -Customers will find the store pleasant and clean
>   -Customers will feel valued

The various statements outlined in the previous version of the job description can all fit under these main headings as activities which might be suggested by management to produce the result:

> RESULT: Sales on clerk's aisle will increase
> SUGGESTED ACTIVITIES:
>   -Keep shelves fully stocked to meet demand
>   -Allocate shelf-space relative to demand
>   -Keep aisle and shelves clean
>   -Recommend special sales to store manager
>   -Mark prices of items clearly
>   -Display merchandise attractively
>   -Maintain sufficient inventory of products
>   -Determine customer buying preferences
>   -Log inventory turnover

Many natural possibilities for team responsibility in modern organizations are not developed. For example, consider a person in a local government agency who is responsible for securing funding for agency activities. To achieve this result, he writes proposals to federal government agencies and private foundations. When the proposal is finished, he gives it to the supervisor of the secretarial pool to be typed.

On the surface, it seems that the proposal writer's job meets all the criteria we have described so far. He is responsible for a worthwhile result (getting money); he has the authority to use his brain in achieving this result; and he gets feedback on how well he has done. He can enjoy a sense of achievement and of control.

On the other hand, the secretary in the typing pool has one of the dreariest jobs imaginable. She has no result to shoot at. Indeed, she may not even know the result the pieces of paper are supposed to produce, thus putting her in a worse situation than the people in the golf story. She has neither individual nor team nor partial responsibility. She has the fourth and worst kind of responsibility, the responsibility for performing activities without relation to any known result. There is no opportunity for her to plan her work; all that is done by her supervisor. Opportunities for recognition related to performance are few. "The thrill of victory" is impossible to experience in such a job—except in the case where she files a grievance against the company or goes on strike.

In reality, of course, the typist plays a crucial—if unrecognized—part in the result of attaining funding. Unless the proposal writer is willing to type the document himself, he really doesn't have total responsibility for this result because it is unlikely that many of his proposals would be taken seriously if they were submitted in hand-written form. The professionalism of his organization would be suspect.

Merely calling the typist's indispensable contribution to her attention is not enough, however, to motivate her, to give her a feeling of control over the result. We need to design things so that she and the proposal writer work as a team. This means the typist should be taken out of the dehumanizing environment of the typing pool and assigned (no doubt among other things) to preparing proposals. She and the proposal writer can then meet prior to each effort to plan what the proposal will say and how it will look. The typist will then know what the proposal is supposed to say and can spot things that make no sense or that don't clearly state what she knows is supposed to be conveyed. Also, she can contribute ideas on the design of the proposal package, how it should be organized, how it should be arrayed on the page, what graphics to use, and other design elements. The proposal then becomes a true team effort, and when the proposal is funded, they can both experience "the thrill of victory" and be recognized, together, for their important contribution.

To summarize this, then, we can distinguish four types of worker responsibility:

---

1. Total, individual responsibility for a result.
2. Team responsibility for a result.
3. Partial responsibility for a result.
4. Responsibility only for performing activities
   without relation to a known result.

The first two types of responsibility motivate the worker by meeting his needs for achievement. The second two do not meet that need and so leave the worker to look elsewhere for satisfaction.

Precision Management

It is important for managers to realize that most workers today do bring a need for a feeling of achievement to the job. If they don't get it through the job, if the job is not designed to allow them to meet this need, they will get the need met anyway. They cannot be stopped from getting this need met. One way they can do so, as previously mentioned, is to take some action against the employer, to file a grievance for example, or to go on strike.

Of these four types of responsibility, total, individual responsibility is the best. It requires the least management effort (management effort is increasingly greater as you move down the scale) and provides the purest satisfaction of the need for achievement. An example of a job description which gives the worker individual responsibility is on the following page. It is a job description for a worker in a juvenile court.

You will note that in addition to the results, the job description includes "suggested activities." These are included to give the worker an idea of the kinds of things he or she might do to achieve the result. They are "suggested" activities, however, to indicate that management is interested in the result, not the activities performed and to allow the worker the flexibility to try out new approaches. By making them suggested, not required, activities, we build in the responsibility for thinking that we want the worker to have.

Prior to the job-redesign effort, this job description included some of the activities on the suggested list, but not all. When the results were defined, the worker's scope of action was automatically broadened. For example, the original job included the duty of "prepare budget each year." To define the result, I asked "Why do we want this done? What is the point?" The somewhat surprising answer the administrator gave to this was "to get the budget approved." I asked, "Would you be willing to give this person the responsibility for that?" After some nervous exploration of this, he saw that to do so would enrich the job and make his job easier by relieving him of many of the activities he had to perform to achieve this result.

You will also notice that the job description indicates how the worker will be measured. This is another crucial element in a

JOB DESCRIPTION FOR ADMINISTRATIVE ASSISTANT

OVERALL GOAL:
The court will run smoothly insofar as fiscal, budgetary, and administrative matters are concerned.

MAJOR RESULTS:
1. Budget will be approved by county commissioners.
   Suggested Activities:
   —Work with Division managers to determine court needs
   —Work with administrator to determine budget priorities
   —Work with administrator on presentation to commissioners
   —Meet with commissioners to determine what they will buy
   Measures:
   —Amount of budget accepted

2. Court will operate within budget.
   Suggested Activities:
   —Code bills to right budget
   —Report budget projections to each manager monthly
   —Issue purchase orders, travel vouchers, service claims, credit cards, etc.
   —Work with county on bookkeeping
   —Collect bail monies
   Measures:
   —Degree of budget overrun or underrun.

3. Court will pass audits.
   Suggested activities:
   —Keep accurate records
   —Be prepared for audits at all times
   —Work with auditors to answer questions where required
   Measures:
   —Number of successful audits

4. Staff will have the supplies they need.
   Suggested Activities:
   —Monitor supplies and order as needed
   —Control distribution of supplies
   —Assess staff needs for supplies
   —Budget for supplies to meet needs
   Measures:
   —Number of staff complaints to supervisor

5. Court will collect accounts in a timely manner.
   Suggested Activities:
   —Bill agencies with detention contracts
   —Contact delinquent accounts
   —Type and post vouchers
   Measures:
   —Number of accounts overdue by more than ninety days

6. Staff will get money due them on time.
   Suggested Activities:
   —Expense checks
   —Payroll
   Measures:
   —Number of late or inaccurate checks

worker getting motivation from the design of the job which we will explore further in chapter three.

Team responsibility also meets the employee's need for achievement. At a typewriter-assembly plant, for example, management replaced the long, 100-person typewriter assembly lines with U-shaped, ten-person mini-lines. Instead of doing one activity 240 times per day, each worker, in view of each other, worked as part of a team to produce a visible end-product. The old, partial responsibility was replaced with team responsibility for improving the number of typewriters produced and the quality of the typewriters (quality being measured by warranty repairs). Consistent with the Precision Management principle of giving the workers the authority for thinking, teams were given great latitude about how they went about producing the typewriter. Each worker was encouraged to develop more efficient means of producing the end product. Also, if one person was having trouble, others could stop what they were doing to lend a hand. No longer was there an inspector at the end of the line; the team was responsible for the quality of its typewriters. When parts ran low, workers could go get them instead of requisitioning them, thus saving paperwork and time. The sense of "teamness" was enhanced by old-hands training rookies and by the fact that each team was being judged in comparison to other teams for quantity and quality of production.

The consequences of designing jobs in this way were astonishing. After an initial drop, productivity rose 35 percent as people adjusted to the new approach. Attrition, a serious problem before the change, fell by 65 percent. Quality increased, morale rose, and costs were reduced.

As the new system took hold, a sense of team spirit took root among the workers. On their own, they began to name their teams, choose team colors, and so on. One team even had a mascot.

Prior to the institution of the team system, each worker had only partial responsibility for a result and hence no sense of achievement. Quality was the quality-control inspector's problem, not theirs, and output per hour was fixed by management, which set the rate on the assembly line based on time-and-motion studies. Those who saw better ways of doing things had no incentive to try to get management to listen or to struggle to get their ideas adopted. Indeed, they had a negative incentive in that one of their few sources of job-related satisfaction was to share stories about how stupid the management was.

Cut off from a sense of achievement in their jobs, the workers may well have devoted a large part of their mental energy to thinking about professional team sports, a favorite baseball or football team, for example. But with the new system, they had teams of their own to "play" on, and they put the same type of effort into making their team "number one" as a professional football team does.

In these ways, The Winning Organization creates jobs in which there is the possibility of "victory." The Winning Organization is staffed by employees who are, in popular parlance, "winners," and you can't have winners unless there is something to win.

Chapter 3

Motivation and Measurement

The Winning Organization insures that it gets the results it wants by giving people clear title to them, as discussed in chapter two, and by measuring how well people do in attempting to achieve them.

For some reason, many managers of the standard school, for all their authoritarian, "hardheaded" demands, are very meek about measuring employee performance in a way that truly holds the employees accountable. Of course, when they give no one responsibility for results, they themselves are the only ones accountable for the success or failure of the enterprise, and this may account for their aversion to finding out if they are succeeding or not.

Managers also resist measuring on the basis of outcomes because they believe their workers will be frustrated if they are measured in this way. As with so much in management, however, the opposite is closer to the truth.

I once consulted with a mental health center that had morale problems with its counselors. The counselors were responsible for providing at least fourteen hours of direct counseling to clients each week, and their performance was measured on this basis. I suggested that if that was indeed what they wanted—fourteen or more hours of counseling—they could save money and do a good turn for less fortunate members of their community by hiring some of the local winos to do that job. I pointed out that for a warm place to sit, a wino would cheerfully talk to their patients for far more than fourteen hours each week and, under the present system of measurement, would be their top performers.

They of course were not very amused by this suggestion, but as I pressed them to tell me why they thought their counselors would do a better job than my winos, they found it difficult to put into words how they would know if a wino did the job well or not. Doing the job well, I submitted, meant that there would be an outcome from the fourteen hours of contact, that their clients would get well (or as they finally put it, "return to independent living in the community"). When one of the staff eventually suggested this, however, the supervisor of counseling reacted very strongly. "You can't hold counselors responsible for that!" he said, almost in horror.

But if not responsible for that, for what? If they are responsible only for putting in a certain number of hours, save the money and hire my winos.

This supervisor's reaction was born of concern that getting clients well is a very difficult thing to do, and that making that a goal and measuring people in comparison to that goal might frustrate and demotivate them. For many of their patients, to be sure, solving their problems might well have been nearly impossible. So instead, he gave the counselors a job a wino can do, and his counseling staff was bored and surly.

The Challenge of Measuring

The point the supervisor was making, of course, was that getting all of those clients well was impossible, and to insist on one hundred percent, perfect performance is unreasonable. Getting all their patients well was as elusive to those counselors as a round of golf in par is to most golfers or a 300 game is to most bowlers. But the fact that a 100 golfer never comes close to shooting par doesn't demotivate him. On the contrary, he practices and tries new things, subscribes to golf magazines, attends golf clinics, watches good golfers on television, and daydreams about golf at work, when he should be doing the paperwork that goes along with his job (perhaps as a bored counselor).

The challenge that motivates him to spend all this money, time, and effort is not to shoot a 72 but to break 100. On each individual hole, he may set out to shoot par, but the total score that will satisfy him is 99. Once he has achieved that, he will set a more ambitious target. In this way, he keeps growing toward the ideal of shooting par.

And if he had a similar challenge at work, he might also try new things and subscribe to professional journals, and attend conferences on counseling and constantly work on perfecting his craft. The goal for each individual patient the counselor advises is the solution of his or her problem, but the target, to be realistic, is something far less than 100 percent.

If that supervisor of counseling were to buy a golf course and were to get worried about the frustration the average golfer must feel at never being able to shoot par, and if he ran the golf course the way he ran his counseling staff, he might organize things the way the Devil did in chapter one. Or he might take the holes out of the course so we could just hit the ball around without worrying about a score. But golfers would then stop coming to this course; they'd be bored. And the only way he could get them even to show up would be to offer them inducements, such as free beer or fancier electric carts—or to pay them to come.

If he did pay them to come, they would certainly stop practicing, trying new things to improve, subscribing to golf magazines, watching good golfers play, and thinking constantly about perfecting their games. They would start to behave the way workers behave when they work under standard management practice.

Tapping the Desire to Grow

A worker's dedication to improving his abilities is the most valuable asset an organization can have. It is a product of two things, the first being that the worker knows the extent to which he is succeeding, just as a golfer does. This means that the worker not only has results for which he is responsible but that he is measured on his performance in achieving them. The second factor is that the worker knows that his manager will regard failure not as a cause for punishment but as an opportunity to help the worker improve. She helps him analyze why his performance was not "up to par" and helps him plan how to do better next time.

The role of the supervisor is thus to help the employee succeed rather than to goad or control him into better performance. This emphasis on growth enables management to tap the full motivational power of measuring performance by results.

By giving workers responsibility for a result and then measuring the degree to which they achieve it, we create a situation in which the worker's own ego and sense of self-worth are inextricably woven into the achievement of organizational objectives. By contrast, in traditional organizations where managers give workers no responsibility and confine them to a narrow set of activities, the worker's own ego and sense of self-worth has no natural outlet on the job. Workers may therefore look for other ways of "winning," such as seeing how little of the spirit and intent of the supervisor's instructions they can carry out.

One of the principal advantages of Precision Management over standard management, therefore, is that the worker's ego and sense of self-worth are working for management rather than against it. Managers have no more powerful resource at their disposal.

American managers of the standard school have spent billions trying to motivate workers by offering various inducements. They've raised salaries, given them more days off and better pension plans and more generous hospital benefits. They've established company soft ball teams and hosted employee picnics. None of these things has worked very well, however, because none of these things changes the job. In fact, to enjoy most of these inducements, you must be away from the job, and if it makes your leisure time more enjoyable, it only makes the job more dismal by comparison.

The first steps in making the job more challenging and rewarding were described in chapter two. In order to make sure that these changes motivate the worker to the greatest extent possible, however, we need to measure the worker's performance to see if she is achieving the results we set out for her. If we don't do this, we run the risk of making the job description a mere piece of paper.

Weaknesses of Standard Performance Appraisal

Standard management does measure workers, but it doesn't measure results. Standard performance reviews are both stressful and meaningless because they either measure personality traits (such as drive, tact, creativity) or whether or not a certain set of activities has been performed. Measurement of personal qualities is always a subjective judgment which can be argued and which can form the basis of successful employee law suits. ("My boss didn't give me a raise because he said my judgment was poor, but he only said this because his judgment is poor, and he can't judge me accurately.") Measurement of whether activities are performed, as with the counselors mentioned earlier, doesn't assess the quality of the performance.

It reminds me of a joke my neighbor pulled on me the other day. He came across the road one evening and said "Hey, I taught my dog to whistle."

"Really," I said. "Gee, I've never seen a dog that can whistle before."

"Oh, well, she didn't learn. But I taught her."

If we were to assess my neighbor's performance in teaching his dog to whistle, we might find that he rated very highly in the terms standard management uses to assess performance. We might find he was very creative and inventive in the methods he employed, that he showed drive and perseverance, that he got along well with others (especially his dog), that he dressed appropriately, and put in more than the minimum number of hours. We might find he was punctual and put forth great effort. He did an outstanding job of teaching his dog to whistle by these criteria.

Precision Management Performance Criteria

Managers employing Precision Management methods might well be concerned about some of these same things. They might counsel my neighbor about his techniques and suggest changes in his methods. But they would be concerned about these things only because they affected the results he was supposed to achieve.

And they would measure his performance in only one way—can the dog whistle or not?

In short, they aren't concerned about whether an employee goes through the right motions or works long hours or exhibits any number of wonderful characteristics. They care only whether he achieves the result for which he is responsible. They don't care if the salesmen they supervise knock on a hundred doors or put ads in the paper; they judge their performance only on whether sales are made. They aren't impressed by a proposal writer who stays up all night for four nights to get a proposal done; they measure her only by whether the proposal is successful. If they get the money, she gets a good rating. If she doesn't, then she didn't do her job, and they should try to find out why and help her do better next time.

This may seem like a pretty tough approach, but I can get winos to write proposals if that's all I'm interested in. The only reason we hire a person—unless we're running a charity program—is to get results, and their success at producing those results is the only meaningful way of measuring them.

The advantages of this approach are illustrated in the following story. A client of mine had a small print shop on the premises which did the copying and printing necessary for all employees' work. The copy center was run by a clerk about whom everyone complained. The clerk didn't seem to care much about his job. He seemed to regard every request as a personal inconvenience. And if he didn't get your printing or copying done on time, well that was your problem, not his. You should have given it to him sooner.

Like many units in large organizations that exist to serve other units, he had the smug security of having a monopoly on their business. If they didn't like it, there was no competing copy center down the hall to go to. He had a little power center, a little empire, and if you were extra nice to him and buttered him up and invited him to your parties and took him out to lunch, he might be disposed to produce only semi-sloppy work in a reasonable amount of time.

Precision Management

Those who complained, needless to say, were always last on his priority list.

His supervisor evaluated him every six months, using the company's evaluation form, and gave him low marks for "Ability to work with others." But, to be honest, they had to give him high marks in many of the other areas on the form, such as appropriate dress, punctuality, and the quantity of his work. So it all averaged out to show him to be satisfactory, and they were stuck with him.

When we installed a Precision Management system, the first problem was to define the results they wanted from him. The result wasn't just copies of things. He did, in fact, produce copies of things. Adding, "in a timely manner" only gave them a performance standard, not a result. What they wanted was good copies, but the problem was how to measure "good."

I asked them how they now, intuitively, knew the copies weren't good. They answered that there was nothing intuitive about it, that you could tell from the howls of angry staff people (the "others" he failed to "get along with"). So I suggested the staff should be the ones to judge the quality of the copies. Even though each staff person may have a different standard, the result stayed the same: satisfy the staff as to the quality and timeliness of the printing. The result was thus written "Other employees will be satisfied with the professional quality and timeliness of the printing," and the problem became one of figuring out how to measure this result.

In such cases, where it is the opinion of others that is the end-product we seek, the easiest way to measure performance is to ask those others. One possible way to measure was the number of requests for printing to be redone, but this was something no one had ever done before because they were afraid of getting on the clerk's "bad list."

The second way of measuring involved a simple, one-third-page form that the clerk printed up and included with each finished printing order. On it were two questions: 1) Are you satisfied with the quality of your printing? and 2) Are you satisfied with the timeliness of your printing? Each question was followed by two boxes, one for yes and one for no. It took employees about five seconds to fill the form out. When they finished, they put it in their out-boxes, and it was automatically routed to the clerk's supervisor, whose secretary tabulated the results.

At each six-month evaluation, the clerk was evaluated on this and other results. Because the data were available to the clerk at all times, he already knew how good his performance was. The performance evaluation interview thus became one in which the supervisor could concentrate on giving praise for improved performance and helping the employee come up with a plan to improve in needed areas. There was no arguing about the rating itself, because it was no longer a matter of the supervisor's subjective judgments; the data were there, unarguable, and clear to all.

This form, even though it was extremely simple to use and took little time, did constitute a new procedure that took some time away from doing the work. In making the decision to use such a measuring device, the question that must be asked is "Is this result important enough to go to the bother of evaluating it?" In the above example, the answer was yes, we do think that one of the most important parts of the clerk's job was that company employees get good copy service. As such, it was important to measure it.

Failing to measure important goals such as this negates the point of setting the goal in the first place. Having no means of telling whether they are succeeding or not, employees in traditional environments lose interest in trying to accomplish their goals.

By contrast, keeping score in this way completely changed the performance and the attitude of the copy center clerk. People tend to achieve that on which they will be measured personally. Because the clerk's performance was going to be measured on the attitude of his "customers" toward his work, he started taking care to make sure he got the instructions right. He started scheduling things efficiently. He started calling up people who often had large printing needs and asking them about upcoming demands so he could be sure to make time for them. He started readjusting the machine when it made bad copies, and keeping the screen of the copying machine clean. He started asking people how he might better serve them.

As a result, the company got better performance from the clerk. And the clerk, in trying to get a better and better score, found that he had a greater sense of involvement in the organization. As his isolation decreased, his sense of job satisfaction increased, and he found his performance did improve. He received bonuses and pay increases and eventually a promotion.

By taking the trouble to define the result and how it was to be measured, management gave the clerk the incentive to perform to his maximum potential. As with the golf situation in chapter one, there was nothing wrong with the clerk. What was wrong was the situation in which he worked. By changing those circumstances (the rules of the game) and defining how the score was to be kept, management brought out the clerk's "winning" characteristics.

This example also shows how it is possible to measure things which at first seem "unmeasurable," such as customer satisfaction. By regularly soliciting the opinions of the people whose satisfaction matters, we can "objectify" this subjective information.

Of course, such a system of measurement won't always change the behavior of the employee. But if the employee is determined not to make a positive contribution, it at least gives management an objective basis for disciplinary action, if necessary.

One city government had particular problems with an employee whose job was to collect garbage. The city policies indicated that for people to get their garbage picked up, citizens had to carry their cans out to the curb. Specifically, the policies stated that cans had to be within five feet of the curb to be eligible for pickup. Also, the cans were not to weigh more than 80 pounds. The problem worker carried a stick with him that was exactly five feet long. Any can that was more than five feet from the curb, even by an inch, he did not empty. He also carried a scale with him, and if the can weighed eighty-one pounds he did not take the garbage.

As you might imagine, the city received a number of complaints from citizens unlucky enough to be on his route. On receipt of these complaints, the worker's supervisor would sometimes write up a formal reprimand. In response, the worker would immediately submit a grievance. The manager of the garbage collection department would always back the supervisor up, but somewhere in the appeal process someone would say that in fact the worker was right, the rules did say the can had to be five feet from the curb and weigh less than 80 pounds, and so he won each grievance. At one point, the city got so many complaints they fired the worker; he sued the city and, armed with the evidence of all his successful grievances, got his job back with back pay.

The city had always regarded this worker as a "loser." But as we analyzed the situation in light of the principles set out in the last chapter, they realized that he was not a loser at all. He was a winner who had nothing to win in his job. His need to win was so great, that he had figured out a way to get it met—by daring management to discipline him and then submitting a grievance. In this arena, he was a winner without peer. He was the Rocky Marciano of garbage collectors. He had never lost.

Accordingly, they redefined the job so there could be something to win. They defined the result as "Citizens will be satisfied with the quality of their garbage collection service." This was to be measured by the number of citizen complaints. (Numbers of complaints is not usually a very good way to gauge satisfaction because in many situations a dissatisfied customer will not go to the trouble of complaining. This is less likely to be true in the case of garbage collection than in other cases, however.)

The supervisor of garbage collection kept track of complaints for each route, and posted the "standings" in plain view. Each month, the entire work force went to a tavern, and the best crew of the month had the honor of having the supervisor buy them all the beer they could drink and pour it for them. He also drove them home.

When this system was instituted, management assumed that their frustrated winner, the problem employee, would see that now there was something to win in the job. Each month, he would have a new chance to win. They also thought that the idea of the supervisor pouring the beer would appeal to his anti-management attitude.

Indeed, this did seem to work for a short time. The employee did see that if he continued his old ways, he would always lose, something he had never done before. But his hostility toward management was so ingrained that eventually he could not, in good conscience, play this game. And so, rather than be a loser, he quit.

Measuring Team Responsibility

In cases where there is team responsibility for results, each member of the team is rated according to how well the team does as a whole. This creates some peer pressure toward top performance.

An example of this comes from a city public works department. This department had an annual plan for all the maintenance work to be done in the city—water mains replaced, pot-holes filled, and so on. Each of these activities was done by a crew. Most workers worked as a part of several crews. Worker A, for example, might work with worker B on patching streets, with worker C on leveling, and with worker D on ditch maintenance. For each crew he got a score. If at the end of the period, for example, he and worker B had achieved 50 percent of the street patching that had been planned for that period, they would each receive a score of 50 for that activity.

Each worker's total score came from a weighted average of activities. To continue the above example, if worker A spent 25 percent of his time during the period on street patching and 75 percent of his time on leveling, his score for leveling would count three times as heavily as that for street patching. If he and worker C achieved 125 percent of plan on leveling, worker A's total score would be 106.25 (125 times 75 percent equals 93.75 plus 50 times 25 percent or 12.5). In examining each worker's score at the end of the period, management could easily identify top performers and those who needed some kind of supervisory intervention.

This particular personnel evaluation system was closely tied in to a system of workload planning, as most useful performance appraisal systems are. Central to the system was a plan for production in each of the maintenance areas. This plan was developed by department foremen, in consultation with the work force, and approved by the director. The plan reflected historical performance data, which served as a standard of satisfactory performance, and seasonal situations, such as the need to do more of certain types of activities in the summer and others in the winter. The plan was typically modified as the year went on to reflect changing conditions. In the event of a flood, for example, or of a particularly severe winter, there might be an increased need for more street patching than had been planned.

The lead man on each crew kept track of the crew's productivity by means of a daily crew card that replaced the time cards (this in itself signalled the change in management's attitude in that what was being measured was no longer sheer time spent but rather productivity). Crew performance was verified by the foreman and, occasionally, by the division supervisor.

When a worker's production was less than planned but more than the historical average for his activities, he or she was regarded as doing a satisfactory job. When the worker's production was less than the historical average, he was regarded as doing an unsatisfactory job unless there was some reason that the plan itself was to do less than the historical average. If the unsatisfactory worker was nonetheless showing improvement in his performance, he was not regarded as a subject for disciplinary action.

Every two weeks, the division supervisor and the foremen received a computer report, telling them what percentage of the plan had been accomplished for each activity under their supervision. Each worker under a foreman's supervision was ranked according to the weighted average of his or her productivity.

Each worker received a computer printout of his individual performance every two weeks also. His printout showed his weighted average and his rank among his coworkers, although it did not mention who ranked above and below him.

One of the bonuses of using this system was that management could easily identify its top performers. With the computer report, management got a ranking every two weeks for both the two week period and for the year to date. A sample form, showing part of what the foreman's printout looked like, is on the next page. Management could use such data to create "Employee of the Month" and "Employee of the Year" awards, based on productivity.

In that example, the foreman's report contains an overall breakdown by the activities under his supervision. It indicates the activity number, the way the productivity is measured (by meters, line feet, complaints, and so forth), the reported vs. planned production for the two-week period just ended, and the percentage of the plan that has been completed to date. The complete printout also contained the planned and year-to-date figures for production per man-hour. For each employee supervised by the foreman, the report listed the activities he or she engaged in during the period, the amount of time spent on each, and the production per man-hour. "Percent of plan" refers to production for the two-week period. In Joe Doer's case, for example, his production was slightly more than the planned production per hour (109 percent of plan). Mr. Doer worked only eight of the ten work days in the period, however, and so the value of his contribution during the period (as opposed to his value per hour on the job) is only 87 percent of the planned production for the two week period.

Because Mr. Doer didn't work on any other activities during the period, his percentage for that activity is the same as the total value. In the other two examples cited, their value is a weighted average of their production on two activities. Ms. Renee's total score, for example, is arrived at by multiplying her production on activity 345 by 40 percent (the percent of her time spent on that activity) and adding that figure (40.96) to 60 percent of her production on the other activity she worked on. The result gives her a total score of 148.96, making her the outstanding worker of the period in this brief example.

Note that her score on activity 345 is exactly the same as that of Mr. Rut. That is because they worked on this activity as a team, and the teams' score is attributed to each of them. Judging by Mr. Rut's performance on the other activity he engaged in that period, it may be that peer pressure from Ms. Renee spurred him to excel

FOREMAN: JOHN DOE

REPORT PERIOD   JUNE 14-JUNE 25

ACTIVITY NUMBER	UNIT OF MEASURE	PRODUCTION/MAN-HOUR REPORT	PERCENT OF PLAN	VALUE OF PERCENT PLAN	PERCENT OF PLAN COMP.
341	Meters	.48		.44	51.8%
345	Ln Ft	1.32		1.67	118.6%
355	Comps	.51		.75	25.3%
357	Locs	1.82		1.25	62.4%

EMPLOYEE: JOE DOER

ACT. NO.	ACTIVITY NAME	DAYS WORKED	PRODUCTION PER HOUR	PERCENT OF PLAN	VALUE OF PERCENT	TOTAL VALUE
341	METER MTCE/REPAIR	8.0	.48	109.09%	87.27	87.27

EMPLOYEE: MELONEY RENEE

ACT. NO.	ACTIVITY NAME	DAYS WORKED	PRODUCTION PER HOUR	PERCENT OF PLAN	VALUE OF PERCENT	TOTAL VALUE
345	SERVICE MTCE/EXC	4.0	1.71	102.39%	40.96	
347	SPOT SERVICE REP.	6.0	.45	180.00%	108.00	148.96

EMPLOYEE: RANDY RUT

ACT NO.	ACTIVITY NAME	DAYS WORKED	PRODUCTION PER HOUR	PERCENT OF PLAN	VALUE OF PERCENT	TOTAL VALUE
345	SERVICE MTCE/EXC	4.0	1.71	102.39%	40.96	
355	COMPLAINTS	6.00	.41	54.67%	32.80	73.76

during the four days he worked with her. Indeed, the experience of those who have tried such a system is that the foreman no longer need play the role of the goad; the employees themselves put far more effective pressure on each other to perform than a supervisor could ever do when they know they are going to be scored as a group.

Results-based systems of measurement lead to a different relationship between the supervisor and the employee. In standard management, the pressure to perform comes from the supervisor. Because it comes from without, employees tend to resist such pressure. It helps them protect their sense of self-worth to resist it. When the employee finds that his performance is going to be measured in a meaningful, objective way, however, the pressure to perform comes from within. In order to protect his sense of self-worth under this type of system, he seeks to perform as well as possible, and when he isn't doing so well he naturally looks for help. The natural place to turn is to the supervisor.

It is not so natural, however, for the supervisor to be able to handle these requests, at least at first. The switch from being a "teller" to a resource is a difficult one to make. Once they are trained in the new system, however, and find how much easier it is to manage in this new way, the supervisors also tend to become more motivated. It is a lot more pleasant to go to work each day knowing your people are internally motivated and knowing they look to you for advice than than it is to have only a daily struggle with unwilling employees to look forward to.

Measuring Supervisory Performance

Supervisors, too, can be measured by results, of course. In one fire department, for example, a result for a first-line supervisor was stated as "all fire fighters in the company will have the skills, knowledge and abilities necessary to respond to fires." To achieve this result, the company officers drilled their people on their knowledge of streets and addresses, conducted physical fitness activities, and held periodic practice sessions on the various skills the fire fighters needed.

One of the ways management found to measure this result was to observe performance in simulated emergency situations. Every six months, the department's training officer would arrive at the station and give the company an address where there was a "fire." The company would respond exactly as in a real emergency but without red-lights and sirens. The training officer would check to see that the fire fighters knew the address (sometimes an obscure location) and check to make sure they took the most direct route. He timed how long it took them to don their breathing apparatus, observed how efficiently they laid their hose, and so forth.

Performance was also observed during actual emergencies, but this simulation had several advantages. First, the training officer could be totally involved in observing what was happening, whereas in an actual emergency the fire was his first priority. Second, the exercise was always debriefed as a learning experience so as to be useful to the fire fighters. The point of measurement is not to punish but to reward or to help people learn to do better.

So far in this chapter, I have given four examples of how performance can be measured. Here are some for you to try. Below are seven statements of results. For each, identify a means of measuring it. (The job title is given in parentheses.)

---

1. (Maid in hotel) Customers will be satisfied with the cleanliness of their rooms.
2. (Cook at senior center) Seniors will get adequate nutrition.
3. (Parole Officer) Youth will learn alternative, positive ways of behaving.
4. (Billing Clerk) The organization will receive all monies to which it is entitled.
5. (Museum Receptionist) Visitors to the museum will feel comfortable and welcome.
6. (Grocery Clerk) Sales on Clerk's aisle will increase.
7. (Grade School Teacher) Students will make reasonable progress in reading.

Precision Management

Since there are always several possible ways of measuring any result, there is no one right answer to each. The means used in the actual cases follow, but think about your own answers before reading on.

1. The first result can be measured by soliciting customer opinions. In this case this was done at check-out, while the customers were waiting for their bills to be printed out. By actively soliciting the opinions, management avoided the problem that customers would register their displeasure simply by not coming back. Measurement was made easier by giving each maid a block of rooms (turf) for which she was totally responsible. Customer responses on the issue of cleanliness (and other factors) were tallied every month to give the employees responsible a score.

2. It took management a long time to figure out an economical way to measure this one. Initially, the measure was defined as the number of center "customers" who were treated for malnutrition. This, however, was hard to track because many such cases might never come to their attention. After defining this as the result they wanted, management realized that the cook needed to be more than just a preparer of meals in order to achieve this result. She became involved in other activities such as teaching a class in preparing low-cost, nutritious meals and teaching seniors about their nutritional needs. After this happened, the measure of this result was defined as the number of seniors who evinced nutritional problems on their health checkups at the center.

3. The measure of this result for the parole officer was the number of youth who committed crimes as juveniles during their parole period.

4. The billing clerk's measure was the number of overdue accounts. As usually happens, giving the clerk a result to achieve rather than an activity to perform, expanded the number of activities he performs. In this case, the clerk's job was expanded from one of merely sending out bills to doing many things necessary to collect the accounts.

5. Management measured the feelings of visitors to the museum by periodically having visitors complete a simple evaluation form. They also measured this result by the number of

visitors who returned, as indicated by their response to the question "Have you been here before?" at reception.

6. This example was alluded to in chapter two. The measure is of course the volume of sales of products from the clerk's aisle. This was first tracked by the reorder of stock. When the store bought automated cash registers, the computer kept track of sales by aisle.

7. The measure of the teacher's performance in this case was the student score on a standardized test administered before and after the school year. In the debate surrounding President Reagan's 1983 suggestion that teachers be paid according to merit, the opposition objected that "one person with one set of methods will be judging another person's methods." This is indeed what often happens when teachers are evaluated. In order to make that evaluation meaningful, the teacher needs to be measured by the results he or she achieves, not on the methods employed.

Setting Targets

Determining how to measure a result is only the first step in the process. The second component in measuring performance is the target. The target says how many or what percentage the employee will try to attain during a given period. For example, the hotel maid might have a target of 95 percent of the customers being satisfied with the cleanliness of their rooms as indicated by their responses on the evaluation cards. Or the billing clerk might aim to collect 50 of the 70 overdue accounts being collected during a given period.

It is the target that keeps the employee's job alive. If we say merely that the grocery clerk's job is to increase sales, the motivational value of the result may fade over time. But when we say that his job is to increase sales by 400 units over the next six months, then we give him a challenge; we give him something to shoot at, something concrete to try to achieve.

The target also keeps the result from being interpreted as an absolute. In the case of the counselors mentioned previously, the result was that their clients would get well. The difficulty of achieving this for more than a very few caused the supervisor to react negatively to holding counselors responsible for this outcome. And, in fact, if we were to demand 100 percent perfect achievement of this result, we would succeed only in frustrating the counselors. By setting a target of, say, getting one client back to independent living in the community this quarter, we do not negate the fact that our goal is to get all clients well, but we give a realistic target the employee.

Targets need not be the same for all employees doing the same job. In the case of the counselors, for example, each one may have several clients who have only mild difficulties and for whom the goal of independent living is relatively easy to achieve. That counselor could have a much higher target than one who has only very severe cases.

Targets should always be proposed by employees. If their supervisor finds the target unacceptably low (or unreasonably high), she can always disapprove the target and ask for a different one. But it is important that the target be set by the employee. The major reason is that employees will tend to resist or resent a target set for them by their supervisor.

Many supervisors are nervous about the level of targets they might get when they ask employees to propose them. But nearly every time they are surprised at how high the employee sets his sights. One of the reasons for this is that people need challenging goals to make their lives rewarding. Also, when we ask an employee to set a target, his sense of self-worth is on the line. If he sets the target ridiculously low, he is publicly branding himself as being incompetent. In fact, the supervisor employing Precision Management methods more often has to disapprove a target for being too high than for being too low. As one supervisor commented, "If I said increase sales by five percent I'd spend the rest of the quarter arguing about why that was unreasonable. Meanwhile, they would prove to me that I was wrong and they were right by failing to meet the target. Now, when I ask them to set a target they think they can achieve, they say seven percent."

In order to help employees feel free to set challenging goals, managers using Precision Management methods must make clear that failure to achieve the target will not be cause for punishment. Rather, the manager's response to failure to reach the target should be the same as a golf coach's response to a player's failure to reach par. He will go over the employee's experience with her, help her see why she didn't reach the target, and help her learn from it so she can do better next time. This process is described in more detail in chapter eight.

In the public works example mentioned previously, the planned production for each of the activities was proposed by the crew responsible for that activity. The crew met, examined the historical production for that activity and proposed a target for the coming year to the Director of Operations. These recommendations were then reviewed by the Director in light of the specific needs of the city. He then approved the target or rejected it as being too low or, in the case where workers on that crew might be involved in another activity of higher priority, too high. If the target was rejected, the workers met again and came up with a new recommendation.

Setting targets makes the manager's job much easier. By knowing what the employee is supposed to achieve and by having both parties agree to the level of performance desired, the employee will perform many of the tasks that traditional supervisors wind up doing, such as deciding things are not going well, deciding on what changes need to be made, and deciding what to do next. If the employee is unsure what to do, he will naturally turn to the supervisor for help. This puts the supervisor in the role of being a resource person rather than being a controller or a goad. This difference is one of the fundamental advantages of Precision Management over standard practice.

This is not to say, however, that the manager should not monitor employee progress toward achieving the target. Neither the employee or the supervisor should ever be taken by surprise that a target has not been reached. The boss should check as often as she feels is necessary to see that the employee is making the required progress. A sample form that some managers use for this purpose is on the following page. It assumes that there will be six checkpoints on the road to completion of the goal. Obvi-

MAJOR RESULT TARGET ON TARGET/OFF TARGET

| | | 1 | 2 | 3 | 4 | 5 | 6 |

ously, there might be more checkpoints if the boss felt it were necessary.

At each checkpoint, the supervisor meets with the employee to review progress and to see if it is on- or off-target. If it is off-target, they analyze the employee's experience in trying to reach the target, and the employee submits a plan (perhaps a few days later) for getting back on track.

The manager may elect to change the target at these meetings if other priorities have arisen or if it appears the original one was unrealistically high or low. Determining how to measure employee progress takes a fair amount of time and management energy. The payoffs in employee morale and ease of management are so enormous, however, that the investment is one of the most valuable a manager can make.

Chapter 4

Streamlining

One of the advantages The Winning Organization has over its competitors is that it is leaner. It has a lower overhead burden because many of the functions its workers perform are done in traditional organizations by additional personnel, usually at the management level. Jobs such as quality control specialist, expediter, and vice president for planning are not found in The Winning Organization. The activities these people fill their days with are either not necessary in The Winning Organization or are done by the workers themselves.

The Winning Organization is also more efficient because it has less need for meetings and other management efforts at coordination. Traditional organizations split responsibility for results and then have to spend a lot of time and effort reassembling that which their inefficient organization has rent asunder—coordinating fragmented efforts, clarifying turf, and dealing with the political battles that inevitably arise when people find the impact of their work can be altered by the performance and the values of others who have a hand in the final outcome. Traditional organizations tend to operate as macrocosmic versions of the golfers in chapter one.

By designing jobs according to the Precision Management principles set forth in the preceding two chapters, effective managers avoid these fragmentation problems and also lay the foundation for streamlining their organizations. Essentially, streamlining means getting the same amount of work done with less administrative and management personnel. As the following example shows, this can be done even in small organizations where there doesn't seem to be much of a problem.

Streamlining in a Small Organization

A small city parks department had a maintenance division that employed 15 full-time people—a director, a secretary, two foremen, an inspector, and ten maintenance workers. In the summer, the department hired 20 additional workers, mostly high-school students, to help out with maintenance of the 30 parks during the time of peak park usage.

Each day, the inspector visited several parks to see what maintenance needed to be done. Near the end of the day, he returned to the office and reported to the director. Together, they prioritized the list and decided which workers would do what the next day.

Dividing the workers into crews was made complicated by the seniority system. The most senior worker was always assigned the most desirable job and the least senior person was always designed the least desirable job (such as rest-room maintenance). All of this meant that the inspector and his boss often worked late to figure all this out.

The next day, the workers reported to work and found out what they were to do that day, who would be supervising them, and in what park or parks they would be working. Ordinarily, there were more than two crews, which meant that the foremen would get one crew started on a task and then go to a different park to get another crew started. In the summer, a foreman might have as many as six crews to supervise.

The foremen's major complaint was that when they returned to a work site they often found the crew sitting in the truck drinking coffee. When they asked why they weren't working, the workers' answer was that they weren't sure how the foreman wanted them to go about a task, or they weren't sure if he wanted a different thing done, or that they were done with the first task and were waiting to be told what to do next. Citizens sometimes complained about seeing people goofing off in this manner. Some employees were found drinking beer instead of coffee and were suspended. The foremen urged their boss to get a budget increase to hire at least one more foreman so they wouldn't be "stretched so thin."

Other problems included absenteeism and constant grievances filed by the workers. Absenteeism caused delays most mornings as the crews needed to be readjusted by the director to accommodate unexpected absences.

The crisis occurred in 1982 when the division's budget was cut by $50,000. Some of this they could save by putting off purchases of new equipment, but the director was faced with the odious prospect of cutting the two least senior maintenance workers. He saw all sorts of morale problems resulting from this, because everyone would have to do the less desirable jobs they had escaped years before.

In many such cases in government, there is a great temptation to punish the public for not providing enough funds. Another park official, for example, might have responded to this situation by saying that due to the budget cuts, rest-rooms would be cleaned only once every two weeks, or that trash would be collected less often. Such a solution not only solves the budget problem but may put enough pressure on the city council that the money is restored.

This director, however, was dedicated to providing necessary services to the public, and he approached the problem from the point of view of continuing to provide services in the face of these cuts. If you were a consultant and were asked for a different solution, what would you recommend? Think about this and about the lessons learned in the previous chapters before you read on.

The first thing to do, of course, is to define the turf of the worker. What is it they could "own"? The answer was that each could own three parks. (It didn't quite work out that way, because some parks were bigger and some were more completely equipped, but this is close enough for purposes of this discussion.)

Next, how can we build into the job the responsibility for thinking? The answer was that each person would be totally responsible for deciding what needed to be done in his park each day in order to keep it safe and attractive. In addition, the team of workers was given responsibility for the complicated task of scheduling equipment (there was only one mower, for example) so that each person could do the things he thought needed doing. Each month the team met to review any scheduling problems in the previous month (evaluating) and to develop a schedule for the coming month (planning). Further, in the summer, each had two high-school students to supervise, which meant deciding how to deploy their work force (organizing).

Once this was done, it became apparent that, far from needing additional foremen, actually none at all were needed. In fact, there was also no need for the inspector, insofar as his previous duties of deciding what needed doing and scheduling work was concerned.

With the cooperation of the parks superintendent, the director was able to transfer the youngest foreman to a supervisory position in a different part of the department. The plan was to give the other foreman the option of early retirement.

The snag in the plan came when the senior foreman refused early retirement, saying that he would like to bump one of the workers and have his own parks to maintain. He felt it would be so satisfying to be able to get something done right and easily, after all his years of frustration, that he'd like to spend his last years in that capacity. Fortunately, the most senior maintenance worker was also near retirement and he did accept the option of retiring early.

At the outset, the director was concerned that those who had worked up to one of the more desirable jobs would resist having to do the less desirable jobs in the parks. As he voiced his concern, however, the second most senior worker spoke up, his voice quaking with emotion. He said "Darrell, I will support whatever you decide, but in my job I make sure all the playground equipment is safe. I have counted. There are 2,014 bolts I have to tighten. I'd love to clean a rest-room now and then."

In the new scheme, the inspector was kept on primarily as a "score-keeper." Each week, he toured the 30 parks and evaluated their appearance according to objective criteria that are too numerous to mention here. He also asked, at random, the opinions of citizens using the parks. He used their input to plan for new equipment or facilities the community wanted in its parks. The division was able to buy more such equipment than it had planned, despite the budget cut, and therefore was able to provide a better service to the town's citizens.

When the parks department tried this solution it found that each worker began to take more pride in his work. Absenteeism dropped almost to zero. The appearance of the parks improved as each worker could point with pride to "my park." Grievances against management disappeared, and a new sense of team spirit was felt. This new attitude came as a welcome surprise to upper management in the department, many of whom had referred to the workers as "the losers." But the problem was not so much that the workers were losers as it was that they had nothing to win in their jobs—with the exception of the daily, ulcer-producing game they played with their foremen. Changing the organizational structure not only led to less need for management effort but to opportunities for workers to experience the pride of achieving something. By following Precision Management principles in redefining the way the work was distributed and defined, better results were achieved with less cost and management effort.

Obviously, streamlining in this way is of paramount importance to those who are in profit-making enterprises. Again, many inefficiencies may be masked by the way the work is structured, even in small organizations.

A small insurance company, for example, had an office in which applications for new policies were received from independent brokers and new policies written. It employed one file clerk, three writers, two checkers, and two calculators. The office was supervised by a Chief Clerk.

Below is the chain of events that happened when a new application was received:

1. The application arrived from the independent agent and was logged in by the file clerk (who doubled as the receptionist).
2. The application was sent to the chief clerk.

3. The chief clerk gave the application a number, made sure everything was in order, and assigned it to a writer to be processed.
4. The writer wrote the policy and sent it to the checker to be checked.
5. The checker checked the writer's work to make sure the written policy accurately reflected the data on the application. If the policy was inaccurate, it was sent back to the writer to be rewritten. If it was satisfactory it was sent to the calculator.
6. The calculator examined the policy and calculated the customer's premium. She then sent it back to the checker to be checked.
7. The checker made sure the calculator's work accurately reflected the coverage. If it was inaccurate, it was sent back to be recalculated. If it was correct, it was sent to the chief clerk.
8. The chief clerk reviewed the finished policy, and if it was all right he assigned it a policy number and sent it to the file clerk.
9. The file clerk filed a copy of the policy and sent another copy to the agent.

All of this took a lot more time than everyone thought it should. Agents complained that it sometimes took three months for them to get a policy back to their customers and were threatening to take their business elsewhere.

Management also thought the process took too long. A consultant was hired to study the process, and he determined that the main problem was that the writer's job took much longer than the other steps in the process. Although there were already more writers than other people, the consultant recommended hiring another.

While this would have indeed speeded up the process, it would also have added considerably to the company's cost of producing a policy, and so management was hopeful of another solution. If you were asked your opinion, what solution would you recommend? Take some time to work it out, based on the Precision Management principles you have learned so far.

One solution was to give each employee—the writers, checkers, and calculators—total responsibility for customers getting prompt and accurate policies. This meant, first, giving each employee turf by making her responsible for all steps in the process for a particular group of policies. ("These are my customers.") They received the application from the Chief Clerk, figured out what needed to be written, called the agent for clarification if necessary (something that the Chief Clerk had done before), calculated the payments, and checked their own work. They then sent it back to the Chief Clerk, who did a final review as always.

Employees' performance was measured in two ways. One was the number of errors discovered by the chief clerk in his final review. As this was not a detailed, step-by-step check, it was possible that some errors might slip through. So the second means of measuring performance was the number of errors reported by customers or agents in the field. Since any error was potentially very costly to the organization, employees were given added incentive to check carefully by having their pay tied to their error rate.

It is important to emphasize that in the event of an error, it was the employee, not the chief clerk, who was held responsible. The chief clerk's review was not quality control but score-keeping.

This new way of operating led to greater employee involvement in their jobs. There was an initial drop in productivity while the writer learned to calculate and the calculator learned to write the policies. But once that period passed, productivity was much higher than it had ever been. With one person responsible for all the operations, no routing was necessary; no partly completed policies were left sitting on desks; no pieces were lost; no meetings were needed between people to clarify the status of particular policies. The increase in efficiency and worker dedication enabled the company to cut through its backlog of pending applications and reduce the amount of time it took to get policies out by more than half. In fact, although the company didn't discharge anyone, managers began to suspect that they had more people than they needed, not less as had previously appeared to be the case.

That example illustrates how streamlining can also take place without affecting the management level. When managers give workers real responsibility for results, people who once were employed for purposes such as quality control can be employed in more productive work. Quality then becomes the responsibility of the individual worker, no one else.

In this case, as in other cases when this approach has been tried, quality actually improved when the quality control person was removed. The reason is that the quality control person is a crutch for the worker. When quality is not the worker's responsibility, he tends not to work as carefully. After all, if the product is sent out in a flawed form, it isn't his fault. At the same time, the quality control person's presence says to the worker that he isn't trusted to do a good job, and this tends to breed resentment toward the company. Further, with only partial responsibility for quality, the worker looses interest in his job and becomes bored. All of this leads to sloppier work than he is capable of producing.

Streamlining by First Line Supervisors

In the examples so far, streamlining was a deliberate effort of top management. It can also take place in individual units at the instigation of the supervisor. In one large legal department, for example, there was a word-processing pool. The system for getting documents typed went like this: the lawyer who wrote the document took it to the supervisor of word-processing and explained the project to her. She then looked to see which of her eight typists had the least to do and explained the assignment to her. This typist was told to type as quickly as possible, without stopping to worry about any errors she might be making. To encourage this, typists were told to type all first drafts with the screens of their word-processors off. If the typist had any questions about the project, she asked the supervisor who asked the lawyer if she didn't know the answer.

When the typist finished the first draft, it was placed in the supervisor's in-basket to be proof-read. When the supervisor got around to it, she proofread the document, correcting what were ordinarily a large number of mistakes, given the emphasis on speed of entry of first drafts. She then gave it to whichever typist was least busy (usually not the one who typed it originally) to be corrected.

As we have seen before, such a system masks several inefficiencies. Although the emphasis was on speed in entering the first draft, it often sat on the supervisor's desk for more than a day before she proofread it. The supervisor had to explain to the typist what the lawyer had already explained to her. And any time the typist had a question which the supervisor couldn't answer, three conversations had to take place (typist to supervisor, supervisor to lawyer, supervisor to typist) instead of one.

The supervisor of the pool increased its efficiency greatly by applying the Precision Management approach. Think about how you would have done this before you read on.

The first step in streamlining this situation was to give each secretary "turf." Each was assigned the work from a particular group of lawyers (this did not rule out helping each other when one typist's lawyers were producing large volumes of work).

The next step was to define the result. It was formulated as "Lawyers will be satisfied with the quality and timeliness of the typist's work." To measure the result, the supervisor devised a form which accompanied the finished products of the pool on which the lawyer could indicate his/her satisfaction. Targets were very high levels of satisfaction in this case, generally above 95 percent.

Once all this was accomplished, the lawyer could talk directly to the typist about the work to be typed. The typist had total responsibility for quality, which meant the supervisor no longer proofread the work. Once this system was instituted, the work got back to the lawyers faster, the supervisor had much more time for other parts of her job, and the typists experienced a greater sense of challenge and interest in their jobs.

So far, we have seen three examples of streamlining in small organizations. The process of streamlining a large organization is the same, but is made more complicated by the fact that the process can be carried out on both small and grand scales. While each unit of a large organization can benefit from streamlining as described above, so the whole organization can be streamlined, with each unit acting as an analogue of the individuals mentioned in the above examples.

Before we go on to an example of how this works, let's look at some of the general principles of streamlining in a large setting.

Principles of Streamlining

Perhaps the most important principle in streamlining a large organization is that the units should be responsible for a product rather than a function, such as purchasing, engineering, or planning. This is one of the most fundamental differences between The Winning Organization and its traditional competitors.

Standard management practice is based on the assumption that functional units are more efficient. It does seem, after all, that one purchasing authority, for example, would be able to get better prices, cut down on interactions with the same vendor, avoid duplication of purchases and so forth. But such organizations pay a monstrous, if hidden, price in inefficiency.

Process-centered or functionally-based organizations create little fiefdoms, none of which is in itself responsible for the products of the company. In order to gain influence over the end-product and acquire a feeling of efficacy, managers and staff of these units tend to vie with those of other units in sometimes vicious political battles, trying to enlarge their territories at the expense of the other units. Such organizations get bogged down in endless meetings to coordinate, to harmonize, and to solve problems of communication that the structure creates. Task forces are formed, staff is hired to expedite matters, and new layers of management are added to try to coordinate and expedite. People in these jobs work long, draining hours, often with the help of large staffs. And they do perform a very important function, to be sure. But it is a function that is totally unnecessary in a product-centered or results-based organization.

A large organization operated on Precision Management principles blends the advantages of bigness with the creative, motivational, and other advantages of small shops. One of the ways it does this is by creating a structure based on product managers, with individual workers totally responsible for the quality and quantity of production.

Such a structure lends itself to decreases in the number of management levels between the top executive the worker who makes the products or provides the services. Add up the number of people who actually do the work in most companies (those who actually make the cars, design the parts, and so on) and then add up the number of people in management, staff, and support positions. The ratio in large organizations is typically weighted heavily in favor of the "non-producing" and, incidentally, highest paid employees. The inefficiency of this large superstructure counteracts and sometimes outweighs the efficiencies of economies of scale which the organization has due to its size. The large, results-centered organization, structured around Precision Management principles, has both the competitive advantage of a lean superstructure and the competitive advantage of economies of scale common to all large organizations.

Another rule of streamlining is that one person should not ordinarily supervise less than ten employees. This rule is frequently violated for good reasons, but it is a goal to which The Winning Organization comes close. New managerial positions are seldom added unless there is an increase in the number of people to supervise that pushes the ratio well above one-to-ten. This is in marked contrast to the traditional organization in which functional departments tend to burgeon, adding people to try to solve the problems their structural inefficiency creates. Each of these new people in turn tends to cause work for other departments, causing them to add new people, and so the organizational pyramid grows taller and taller, adding more and more cost to products and services.

Workers in such organizations frequently ask, among themselves, "What do they need all those people in the suits for?" It frustrates them when they see new people being hired in these areas while the company becomes less competitive and is forced to reduce its workforce because of slumping sales.

The Winning Organization is able to avoid such a structure because real responsibility for results rests at the lowest possible level. As a result, workers need less supervision. Managers who supervise supervisors are not mere conduits for orders from an overworked and out-of-touch top; they too are responsible for real results and typically have the authority to organize the workforce as they see fit so long as the results are produced. In such an organization, the justification for further levels of management falls away rapidly as you go up the pyramid from the worker level. The results-based organization thus does not suffer from the management and administrative overload of its less effective counterparts.

Two examples of this are given below. Each is based on fact, but is simplified because the real cases were more complicated than they need be to make the point.

Streamlining in a Large Organization

On the next page is an organization chart for a plant of a traditional manufacturer. The products involved are various sizes and models of custom-built, luxury boats. Except for some clerical staff at the upper echelons, only the supervisory personnel are shown on the chart.

The plant manager spent much of his time dealing with his superior and the staff at the home office. As demands from that quarter increased, he added the executive assistant to get information for headquarters on production, labor relations, community involvement of managers, and so forth.

The deputy plant manager handled day-to-day supervision of the other managers in the plant, each of whom controlled a functional unit. Friction was high among these supervisors. There was particular animosity between the manager of assembly and almost all the personnel in the engineering department (also known as "the baboons" by workers in the plant). The manager of assembly complained that the drawings produced by the engineering people were either of no use or caused unnecessary difficulty for the assemblers. To this the manager of engineering retorted that his workers were highly skilled and worked hard,

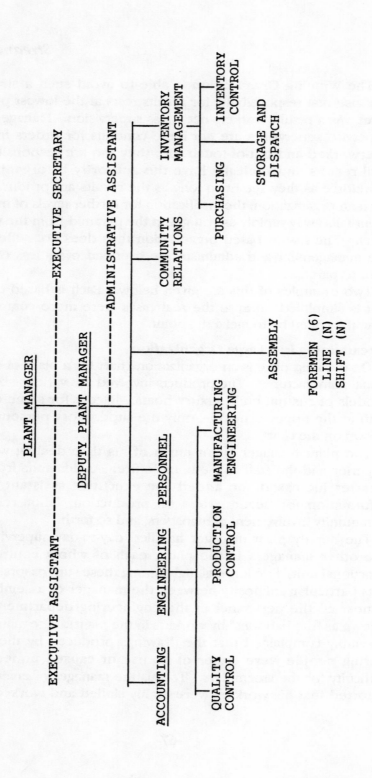

and that the idiots in assembly obviously knew little about good engineering. Engineers complained that the assembly personnel couldn't follow the simplest drawings and instructions. Production control, which scheduled the assembly of each boat, typically caused what the assembly manager thought was unnecessary overtime, punctuated by layoffs and delays. It was further the assembly manager's opinion that he should supervise the quality control unit.

Other frictions occurred between the inventory management unit and the assembly unit, which frequently complained about delays caused by the unavailability of parts. Inventory management, in turn, accused the assemblers of inordinate waste and of theft. Nobody much liked the personnel department.

The plant had enough business to run two shifts on each line. This also created friction because the shifts were constantly complaining that the previous shift had screwed up that shift's work or done something stupid, like putting in the deck before the plumbing was finished.

These units were like the golfers in chapter one, who pointed the finger of blame at each other when something went wrong. The source of all this friction was that no one had responsibility for the final product. To solve that problem, a product-centered organizational structure had to be built within the plant. One way in which this can be accomplished is shown on the next page. The products referred to are the three lengths of boats they built.

You will note that this form of organization requires a smaller superstructure than the old one. The obvious question, then, is: what happened to all those jobs that were so necessary before?

The quality control function, as you might guess from the previous discussion, was eliminated as a separate department. The workers were told that they were responsible for the quality of the boats and that they would be measured on this by the number of warranty repairs and the number of customer complaints received about workmanship. As before, two boats were being built on each line, one on each shift. Workers on each shift had team responsibility for quality and speed of construction of their boats.

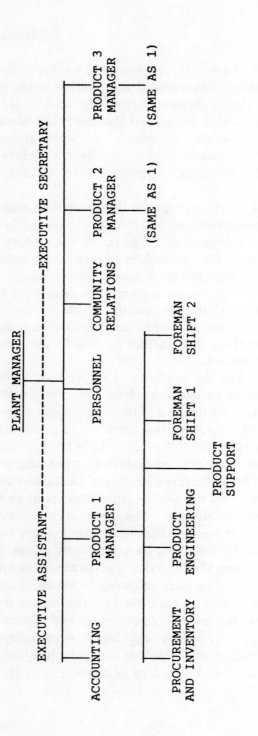

PLANT MANAGER --------- EXECUTIVE SECRETARY

EXECUTIVE ASSISTANT

ACCOUNTING

PROCUREMENT AND INVENTORY

PRODUCT 1 MANAGER

PRODUCT ENGINEERING

PRODUCT SUPPORT

PERSONNEL

FOREMAN SHIFT 1

FOREMAN SHIFT 2

COMMUNITY RELATIONS

PRODUCT 2 MANAGER

(SAME AS 1)

PRODUCT 3 MANAGER

(SAME AS 1)

This allowed any flaws in the construction or any undue delay in delivery to be traced to the team that built a particular boat.

The procurement and inventory functions for each type of boat were placed under each product manager, as were all functions related to building the type of boat the managers, sections were responsible for. While this meant that vendors of items used on all three models had to talk to three people instead of one as in the past, they appreciated the fact that they were talking to someone who was connected to the end product. Each procurement and inventory manager was responsible for making sure there were adequate parts for "his boats." Incidentally, when the company began this new system, it found that the previous inventory management department had been stocking for years items that the engineering department had decided years before not to use anymore. Such waste could not occur under the new system in which the procurement and inventory manager was responsible to a product manager for the parts of one type of boat only.

The production control function, which consisted primarily of scheduling boats on the various production lines, became unnecessary now that each line and each shift no longer worked on a variety of boats. Scheduling production was done by the individual product managers.

Manufacturing engineering, which made alterations in the basic plans to meet customer needs or to improve the overall design, was replaced by product engineering. One person performed this function for each type of boat, becoming familiar with that type and with the problems the workers had assembling it. Instead of being housed in an office building far from the plant, the product engineers were moved to the plant itself and spent a great deal of time on the floor, often helping the workers in the manufacturing process when things were slow. The company thus got better-informed engineering work than ever before.

Storage and dispatch, essentially a warehousing function, was replaced by the procurement and inventory units on the one hand and by the workers themselves on the other. Whenever a worker needed something from the warehouse, they were free to go to the section allocated to their product and get it rather than filling out a requisition as before. This saved lots of paperwork and delays.

The deputy plant manager's job was eliminated because things went much more smoothly now. Each product manager ran his own little boat-building enterprise. product managers were easy to supervise because they had the authority and responsibility to proceed, being measured regularly on the quality and quantity of the boats they produced. Because the reorganization was part of a company-wide streamlining effort, the plant manager was also less frequently bothered by the main office—though not so much less often that he could afford to eliminate the job of executive assistant.

Under the new structure, the role of the personnel department also changed. The number of employees in the department was reduced to accommodate its new role of advocate for the implementation of company policies, such as affirmative action. It also took on a more active training role. The hiring function was now handled by the managers of the various units.

To end our discussion of streamlining, lets take a simplified view of the effect of the above program on the head office of the boat-building company. The diagram on the next page shows, in simplified form, what the headquarters office looked like before the streamlining effort.

As in many organizations, there are an awful lot of vice presidents here. In this company, however, the functional boundaries at the senior vice president level were at least relatively distinct. There were thus fewer cases in which their responsibilities touched, and hence fewer cases in which conflict arose. One case in which this did happen involved the vice president for product support, a customer service that dealt with customers who had problems with their boats or wanted modifications made to them after the sale. The senior vice president for external relations wanted product support to be part of his fief because it related to the customers of the company and had an affect on sales and marketing, while the senior vice president for engineering wanted the unit to remain under

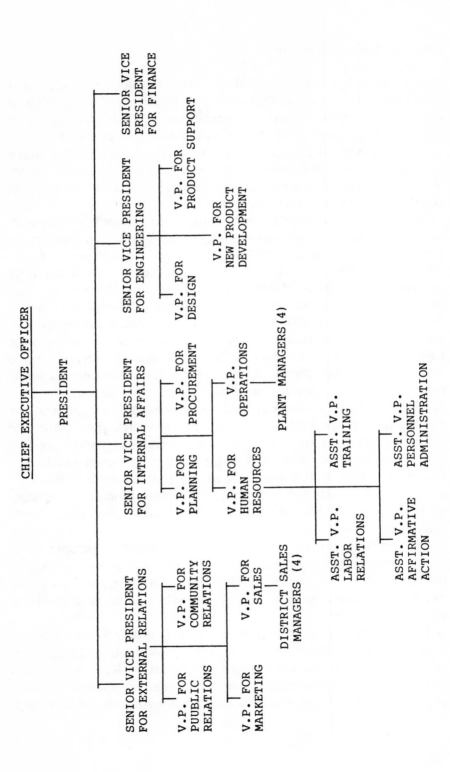

CHIEF EXECUTIVE OFFICER

PRESIDENT

SENIOR VICE PRESIDENT FOR EXTERNAL RELATIONS

SENIOR VICE PRESIDENT FOR INTERNAL AFFAIRS

SENIOR VICE PRESIDENT FOR ENGINEERING

SENIOR VICE PRESIDENT FOR FINANCE

V.P. FOR PUBLIC RELATIONS

V.P. FOR COMMUNITY RELATIONS

V.P. FOR MARKETING

V.P. FOR SALES

DISTRICT SALES MANAGERS (4)

V.P. FOR PLANNING

V.P. FOR PROCUREMENT

V.P. FOR HUMAN RESOURCES

V.P. OPERATIONS

PLANT MANAGERS (4)

ASST. V.P. LABOR RELATIONS

ASST. V.P. TRAINING

ASST. V.P. AFFIRMATIVE ACTION

ASST. V.P. PERSONNEL ADMINISTRATION

V.P. FOR DESIGN

V.P. FOR PRODUCT SUPPORT

V.P. FOR NEW PRODUCT DEVELOPMENT

engineering because it often involved design of mechanical problems, which engineering saw as its province. Other conflicts occasionally arose between procurement and design, between planning and finance, and between sales and operations—the latter over promises to customers about delivery dates the plant managers found unreasonable. (Because of the functional structure, it also took a long time for the plant manager to find out that the delivery date was unreasonable.)

Most of the turf battles were fought within each senior vice president's domain. procurement and operations were constantly at war, particularly since each plant had its own purchasing officer. Similar battles were fought between labor relations and operations, between design and new product development, between public relations and community relations (the latter thought the former should confine itself to advertising, while the former advocated that the latter confine itself to supporting United Way) and between planning and almost everyone else. Planning, as in most organizations where it is broken out as a separate function, consumed a large number of man-hours and produced a large number of documents which were ignored by everyone. To remedy this situation, the vice president for planning wanted to create an assistant vice president for evaluation who would report to him and who would grade the efforts of others in following the plan. This, of course, was opposed by every other department, particularly human resources, which jealously guarded its responsibility for personnel evaluation.

Such battles are the inevitable result of giving people only partial responsibility. In this case, as in others, this set-up drained the productive energies of these very highly paid people, producing more stress and frustration than worthwhile accomplishments.

The success of streamlining the plants and the sales offices made it easier to streamline the administrative level. The guiding principles were to provide at the headquarters level only those things that the local operations could not do themselves, to organize divisions in the headquarters office around whole products, and to reduce the layers of bureaucracy. The final result of these efforts is shown on the following page.

The philosophy behind streamlining at the plants was to make the plant managers feel that they were running their own businesses and, furthermore, to make the product managers feel as if they were running their own small plants. Once that job was finished at the plants, the following changes could be made at headquarters.

The external relations division was given the result "Increase sales of current products" and renamed the sales division. One of the benefits of redefining the mission of this division was that the community-relations function was confined, insofar as headquarters was concerned, to the city in which the home office was located. Prior to this, the vice president for community relations had formulated policies and strategies for the other communities in which the company had plants or sales offices. He then expected reports from the plant manager on the effectiveness of the local community relations efforts. These reports were among the many burdens lifted from the plant manager in the restructuring that enabled him to manage the plant himself, rather than leaving that to a deputy. Now, community relations at the local level became the responsibility of the local managers, with their result in this area being stated as "the community-at-large will value the company." At the headquarters level, the community relations function was assumed by a staff person in the CEO's office.

Marketing and public relations were then combined under the supervision of a vice president for advertising. The market research function was transferred elsewhere, as will be explained below.

With this new, streamlined structure, the senior vice president in charge of sales could supervise the nine district sales managers directly and, in turn, report directly to the Chief Executive Officer. Both of these new reporting relationships were made possible by the greater ability to supervise many people that managers employing Precision Management techniques enjoy. The CEO managed the senior vice president for sales, for example, by giving him total responsibility for the result of increasing sales. Each

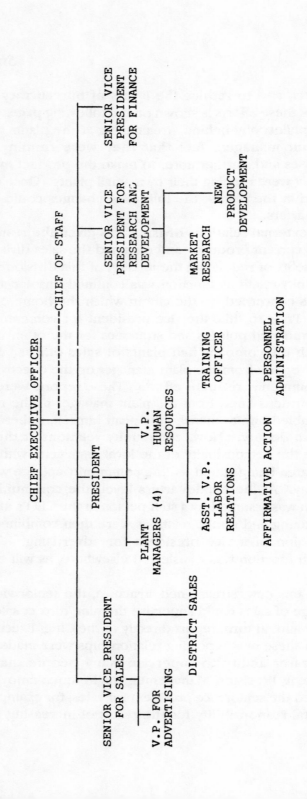

CHIEF EXECUTIVE OFFICER

CHIEF OF STAFF

PRESIDENT

SENIOR VICE PRESIDENT FOR SALES

V.P. FOR ADVERTISING

DISTRICT SALES

PLANT MANAGERS (4)

V.P. HUMAN RESOURCES

ASST. V.P. LABOR RELATIONS

TRAINING OFFICER

AFFIRMATIVE ACTION

PERSONNEL ADMINISTRATION

SENIOR VICE PRESIDENT FOR RESEARCH AND DEVELOPMENT

MARKET RESEARCH

NEW PRODUCT DEVELOPMENT

SENIOR VICE PRESIDENT FOR FINANCE

quarter, they met to discuss the number of sales in the previous quarter, to analyze that performance, and to set targets and plans for the next one. As will be explained in subsequent chapters, the CEO's interactions with all the people he supervised could afford to be relatively infrequent because each was measured on the results for which he or she was totally responsible.

The planning function was eliminated from headquarters as planning became, in accordance with Precision Management principles, the responsibility of those carrying out the plan. Procurement was likewise removed as a home office function, with purchasing responsibility fixed in the plants themselves. As with community relations, the procurement presence in the home office was a source of constant communication and reporting for Plant Managers. Under the new structure, they had more time for actually managing the operation of their factories.

Human Resources retained much the same outward structure as before, but its role changed. The assistant vice president for training, for example, had in the past developed training programs for personnel at all levels. He then, naturally, wanted an accounting of what had happened in implementing these programs, another source of paperwork for upper management at the plant level. Following the Precision Management principle of placing responsibility for a task at the point closest to it, management placed the responsibility for training factory personnel at either the supervisory level or in the personnel office in the plants. Sales training likewise became the responsibility of the district sales manager. The headquarters training unit now concentrated on management training, a function more suited to the home office.

Similarly, labor relations, which used to send blizzards of memo's to the plants, now was confined, with a reduced staff, to negotiating labor contracts. The day-to-day morale of the workers was the responsibility of their supervisors, who were measured on this basis. The affirmative action group continued to make policy in that area, but implementation was now in the hands of the plant administration, with the personnel office playing an advocate role.

Although headquarters had previously been filled with very busy people who worked late hours, they now managed to get more done with fewer people. Under the old system, much time and effort had been spent coping with the cumbersome structure. Additionally, the structure had led each office to make work for the others. It is natural for people to want to feel useful, and if there are no important things for them to do, they will invent things for themselves to do. These things often make work for others, which is why an overstaffed organization often feels understaffed.

As the burden of management activity at headquarters was reduced, the chief executive officer was able to supervise more than the one person, not counting his staff, he had supervised previously. The president was thus put in direct charge of both human resources and the four plants. The need for a senior vice president for internal affairs was eliminated, with the president taking on the responsibility for supervising "the guts of the company." With planning and procurement also gone from this division, it became feasible for the plant managers to report to the president directly. The restructuring thus removed two meddlesome layers of bureaucracy that had existed between the factories and upper management of the company.

The senior vice president for research and development was charged with achieving the result, "Develop new products that people will buy and that can be sold at a profit." His two departments were thus new product development, which included the old department of that name plus the old design department, and market research, which had formerly been under the vice president for marketing under the senior vice president for external relations. Market research was put here because it was necessary to achieving the result. It no longer belonged in the sales department because that department now dealt only with increasing sales of present products.

The most radical change of all was that product support, formerly a department headed by a vice president was moved to the plant level under the product manager. This person knew the products better than anyone at headquarters could because he was involved with the product on a day-to-day basis and had direct access to the builders and engineers who worked on it. Dealers or customers were thus better served by this function.

The finance division was left unaltered by the streamlining effort. Precision Management theory is in many ways at odds with good accounting practice, in that the accounting theory of incompatible functions prevents individuals or teams from having total responsibility for a result. In order to reduce the likelihood of people embezzling money, accounting theory demands that people work at partial responsibility.

It may be, in fact, that the reason so many jobs are designed to give people only partial responsibility is that most business schools have a strong accounting focus. Graduates of those schools may have applied those theories to managing people in other sorts of jobs. In any case, while partial responsibility may be necessary for parts of some jobs in financial units, it is a drag on the momentum of other units of an organization.

Reducing the number of staff (as opposed to line) positions was made possible because the product-based structure led to less need for communication and for expediting work that had been stalled on the desk of someone who had only partial responsibility for the end product. Reduction of staff had an added benefit. Cut off, by the nature of their jobs, from a direct relationship with the building of the boats, staff had sought to meet their needs to feel useful by doing things which would evaluate the effectiveness of line workers and "help" them do a better job. These useful activities caused more work for the line employees, thus reducing the efficiency of the organization and leading to the feeling that additional line personnel needed to be hired. Hiring additional personnel to do the same amount of "real" work, led to increasing fragmentation of the work to be done. These additional line personnel, having only partial responsibility for a result, got frustrated at the smallness of their responsibility. This frustration at the difficulty of getting anything done led to the hiring of new staff people to expedite communication and to coordinate that which the organizational structure had fragmented.

Shortening the Chain

In shortening the length of the chain of command and simultaneously placing decision-making responsibility at or closer to the level at which the work is done, management not only reduces overhead but creates opportunities for more worker motivation and greater organizational effectiveness. This is because traditional chains of command are meant to work in one direction only. They are meant to relay orders, policies, goals, and procedures from the top. In today's ever-changing world, however, the person at the bottom of the pyramid is often the first or only person to spot a problem or an opportunity for the organization.

A simple example of this comes from a large airport fire department. A fire-fighter in the dispatch unit realized that the information in the dispatch book was out of date, that several of the airport tenants had moved and that new tenants had come in. This was information he knew well, because he was the one who used the book each day. The chief, on the other hand, was removed by five levels of bureaucracy from this worker. He was not likely to know this problem existed until a crisis occurred.

If the organization were a traditional one, where all decisions were made at the top, the fire-fighter would have to get approval of his recommendation that the book be updated from four other people before it got to the chief. Each of these intervening people would have the recommendation explained to him by someone unfamiliar with the problem, and each would consider it, review it, let it sit on his desk for a while. The fire-fighter during this time, would get discouraged that his recommendation had vanished into a vacuum. Indeed, if the recommendation were turned down at a higher level, the fire-fighter might not get any feedback on this. Traditional organizations thus suffer because they are designed to facilitate a downward flow of information, a design that discourages worker recommendation and initiative.

In a results-oriented structure, these problems do not occur. The dispatch person would have clear responsibility for the result of making sure that fire-fighters would arrive quickly at the scene of an emergency. He would either have the authority to take whatever action was necessary or to recommend action to his supervisor who would have final authority to approve or disapprove the request.

As the brief examples in this chapter show, once managers design jobs according to Precision Management principles, they can readily streamline the organization and make it much more cost effective.

Chapter 5

The Time Management System

In The Winning Organization, everyone gets the greatest impact from his or her time. By employing the Precision Management principles discussed elsewhere in this book and by using a proven, basic, time management system, employees of The Winning Organization suffer less stress, provide more output per dollar, and, above all, are able to see what the future is becoming and to grasp its opportunities.

Monthly Planning

Because employees are responsible for planning and evaluating as well as doing their work, each employee is able to create daily and monthly plans for accomplishing work that will make a difference, that will get the organization somewhere. The monthly plan starts with each employee's examining the major results for which he or she is responsible. These include results from the job description, temporary responsibilities that have been delegated to them, and results they successfully proposed themselves.

The employee then chooses the targets that he considers to have the highest priority during the upcoming month. These results should answer the question "Why does my job exist?" in that month. The targets chosen are those that will have the greatest impact on the the organization's long-term health and prosperity.

Once the employee identifies the top-priority targets, he decides what he should be able to accomplish within each target in the upcoming month. These short term goals—which may be proposed to the supervisor to make sure they are satisfactory—form the basis for the employee's daily planning. Based on these planned accomplishments, he then gives each target a time budget. For example, he may allot four days to one result, twelve to another, two to a third, and one to the last. These are blocked off on a calendar for the month, indicating what is planned to be accomplished each day. Changing circumstances may alter this plan substantially, of course.

Daily Planning

Daily planning is facilitated by use of the form on the following page. On the left hand side, the employee lists the activities that she will consider doing on that day. This list contains activities that further the accomplishment of monthly objectives and other activities that have come up since the monthly plan was made.

After the list is compiled, the next step is to set priorities. In traditional workplaces, few employees set priorities at all. Most end up spending a great deal of time on activities that are not very important. Even when they do consider the question of priorities, they tend to set them differently than those in The Winning Organization. Most people tend to place first priority on the task that is due first, second priority on the task that is due second, and so on.

The organization suffers when people set their priorities in this way. For one thing, this method puts a premium on short-term projects, and it is most often the long-term projects that are the progressive, future-oriented tasks that keep the organization viable, that enable it to respond to emerging developments in its field and to take advantage of them quickly. As a result, organizations in which people work according to deadline pressure tend to be continually surprised by new developments and slow to respond to them, if indeed they respond at all.

The second toll deadline-based prioritizing takes on the organization is that many important projects may have no deadlines at all. These may be projects that are designed to improve things, for example, or employee-initiated tasks that no one is demanding by a certain date. When people set their priorities on the basis of

TO DO TODAY   SCHEDULE

7

8

9

10

11

12

1

2

3

4

5

NIGHT

what is due first, therefore, these tasks will be last on the list every day. As a result, we find the employees talking wistfully about that project they will get to "some day." Some day, things will really improve when they get to those things. But "someday" is not a day that ever appears on any calendar. And on every real day, there are always tasks that are due tomorrow or next week or next month that take precedence, leaving the organization bogged down in ancient and creaking procedures, their dreams of "some day" becoming drier and more weightless with the years.

A third problem is that even trivial items can have deadlines. The fact that a task is due tomorrow doesn't necessarily mean it's worth doing at all.

But the ordinary worker in the traditional organization has a hard time spotting trivial items. His job is defined in terms of activities, and any additional tasks he is given are phrased in terms of activities also. He tends then to become the victim of what I call Odiorne's law (after George Odiorne from whom I first heard it) which states that "People get so bogged down in activities that they tend to lose sight of their purpose." And when people lose sight of their purpose, they find it impossible to set priorities on any basis other than due-dates. The traditional organization thus cripples itself unintentionally when it fails to define the outcomes or results it expects of its people.

Every employee in The Winning Organization knows what his purpose is and that he is responsible, either individually or as part of a team, for accomplishing certain results. As a consequence, each person can set priorities in two steps, on the basis of impact first, and on the basis of deadlines only after the important tasks have been identified.

Try using the form on the previous page as we go along so that you can become familiar with the system by seeing how it works in your situation. Take some time and identify the top priority targets you will try to meet or make significant progress toward during the next month. Then decide what you will accomplish within each target if you will not complete it during the month. Next, make a list of the things you might do tomorrow, including (but not limited to) tasks you might do that will help you make progress toward the achievement of those targets. Once you have done this, the next step is to set priorities, as described below.

Setting Priorities

The first step in setting priorities is to sort out the important things, the tasks that have a great deal of impact, from those that do not. In doing this, we will give each task on your list a grade of A, B, or C. You may have heard of this before, but my definitions of each of these three priorities is somewhat different than others so you might read on, even if you are a graduate of someone else's time management course.

An A priority is a high-impact task. This is true in my system, regardless of when it is due. A task that will be an A a month from now is still an A today.

C priorities are tasks that don't make much of a difference if they are done or not. If you do them, the organization isn't going to be much better off, and if you don't do them the organization isn't going to suffer. Again, the priority is granted on an absolute basis. A high-impact task which doesn't really have to be done today because it isn't due for two months is NOT a C priority on today's list; it is an A.

B priorities are those tasks that you can't decide about. They really aren't high-impact tasks, but they do produce some results. This, then, is a middle category for tasks that fall between.

In deciding whether an item is an A, a B, or a C, ask these questions:

1. Is this task going to help me make progress toward the accomplishment of my most important targets for this month? If the answer to this question is yes, then the task is an A.
2. Will this activity in some other way help me achieve the results this organization needs from me? If the answer is yes, it's an A. If the answer is no, it's probably a C. If the answer is "I don't know," give it a B, or check it with your boss. (We will talk more about the boss's role in all this later.)
3. What will happen if I don't do this at all? This is perhaps

the most critical question. If the answer to that is "nothing much," and you're pretty sure the organization isn't going to lose an important opportunity by your not doing this, then it is a C priority. If the answer is that although the task is of no value to the organization, the organization will be punished by an outside source (such as a funding source or the government), then the task is a B priority.

4. Do I have to do this so often? Some people do tasks that, while important, do not need to be done with the frequency they are being done. Some school teachers, for example, grade students' spelling tests every day. While it is important for children to have grades in spelling, nothing will change if three-fourths of the papers are graded by the students themselves and not recorded by the teacher.

5. Who is expecting me to do this? This is an important question in traditional organizations. If the organization is structured along functional lines, people need to do tasks which aren't important to their job but are important to another person's job. In such circumstances, I may work on a C priority task that is necessary for you to do your A priority so that in the future, when the roles are reversed, you will do the same favor for me. In The Winning Organization, however, there is little or no need for this consideration. Since people's jobs are designed around whole products, the likelihood of one person having to do a task of low personal priority in order to benefit another worker is very small.

Perhaps the hardest thing to do in all of this is to identify a C priority task. This is something most people find enormously difficult, mainly I think, because the human mind is a marvelously creative and inventive instrument, and it can almost always come up with a justification as to why almost any activity is a useful thing to do. And when a case can be made that an activity is useful, it is hard to see that it isn't very important.

I once did an experiment on this at a workshop I was conducting. I broke the participants into groups of six, and gave each the task of coming up with a justification for why we should stop what we were doing and go through the carpet on our hands and knees looking for needles.

There was, as you might suspect, a lot of grumbling about doing this, but once they got into their discussions, it was amazing what they came up with. One man said, for example, "What if some little kid came in here barefoot and stepped on one of those needles, or what if somebody tripped and fell on one of them, then wouldn't you wish you'd taken the time to look?" After they reported, it took a while for them to settle down and get back to the topic of the workshop because they had come up with such convincing arguments that they should be down on the carpet instead.

In our jobs, we do lots of things because they are similarly useful. Some typical examples include:

—files that are maintained, even though no one ever uses them;

—staff meetings that are held because we always meet at this time each week, even though there is nothing very important to discuss;

—developing a policy for an unlikely contingency and which everyone will ignore anyway;

—reading organizational junk mail;

—the Watergate burglary;

—responding to requests for "input," even when you have none to give.

Many times C priority tasks are so small that we don't even realize we do them when we analyze our time usage. Other times, however, they are so big that we can't see how anything that time-consuming could possibly be a C priority. An example of this was given me by the dean of a department at a large college. Every week he spent three hours with a woman from the budget office going over the printout of charges to his department to make sure it was accurate. When I asked him what would happen if he stopped doing that, he said he guessed it might be possible that he would overspend his budget. I said that that sounded like a pretty important matter to me and asked him what would happen if he went over budget. He said "That's just it. Nothing happens if you go over budget." So he told the woman from the budget office to do the best she could, to feel free to call on him if she saw anything suspicious, and now he has three extra hours every week to do the important work of his department.

Because C priority tasks are hard to spot, you might try thinking of them this way. You've probably had the experience of having a task to do that for one reason or another got put off. You mislaid it, or a crisis occurred, or you got sick, or it got lost in the blizzard of paper on your desk. When you got around to doing it, you realized that the need to do this at all had just gone away. It was due on Tuesday, nobody did it, and nobody cares. If we can spot these things in advance, if we can identify tasks that, while useful, actually contribute little to the results of the organization (and which have no particular negative consequence if not done) we can save ourselves a lot of time, maybe as much as a whole day a week.

In The Winning Organization, people have more time to pursue important results partly because they leave these low-priority tasks undone. Managers are not concerned that the employee does every task possible. Rather they are concerned with the impact of the tasks the employee does do. If employees are working on tasks that produce no results, it is a danger sign. Employees are trained to recognize that and to stop and ask themselves, "Is there something else I could do which would have more impact on the viability of the organization, on the profitability of the company, on our ability to serve our citizens or clients?" If the employee is spending salaried time on a C priority instead of doing these things, he is stealing money from the organization as surely as if he embezzled it.

When you prioritize your list, it is not unusual to find few or no C priority items. This is partly because in making the list we tend not to include these, knowing that they aren't very important. It can also happen because we are too close to the situation, however, and can't see that the item doesn't really have to be done.

So take a hard look at the items on your list. Are they really going to get you and your organization somewhere?

Take some time now and go through your list. In the skinny column on the left side of the form, give each item an A a B or a C.

The first step in the prioritizing process enables us to sort out the high-impact tasks. Now that we have them identified, we want to do those first that are due first. Here, then, is where deadlines come into play.

The second step in the process is therefore to rank your A priorities. We do this according to the deadline and according to the monthly schedule. If our most important short-term goal was budgeted for 12 days, and if today is one of those 12, then activities related to accomplishing that result will get a high priority on today's schedule. All else being equal, they would be A-1, A-2, and so on. If, however, some other high-impact task, not related to that result, is due tomorrow, then it may be A-1, and the others, which may have no due date or a distant one, will be A-2 and A-3.

Go through your list now and rank your A's, one, two, three and so on. If you have relatively few A's, you might do the same with your B's.

By using this system, employees of The Winning Organization always know what the most important thing to do is. And they then spend all of their time working on that. As a result, their impact is greater than that of employees who don't set their priorities in this way.

Prioritizing alone isn't enough, however. Employees in The Winning Organization go further to make sure that they are not only working on the most important task possible but that they are working on it as efficiently as possible.

Prioritizing itself does increase efficiency somewhat. One of the ways people in traditional workplaces lose time is that they work on one thing until they get tired of it, then work on something else until a third thing occurs to them, work on that until the phone rings, leading them to a fourth project that they work on until a crisis arises, and so on. At the end of the day, they leave behind five or six partly completed tasks. This would be all right if, when they came back to the task, they could pick up right where they left off. But it takes time to get back into the train of thought they were in when they were interrupted—or when they interrupted themselves.

People who work according to priorities don't have this problem. They work on one thing until it is finished, then move on to the next task. If one project will take several days to complete, and if there are other high-impact tasks that are due in the meantime, they break the big task down into discrete parts. This enables them to complete a whole segment, a whole unit of thought, then go on to the other tasks. The next day, when they come back to the first project, they can begin on the next segment without having to figure out where yesterday's train of thought was heading.

Nonetheless, prioritizing is primarily a way to gain effectiveness, not efficiency. If the top priority task is not due for a few days, it is easy to work on it at a very slow pace. It is easy, once you get the hang of it, to drag out an A-1 project that would only take two hours at top speed so that it lasts all day.

Scheduling

It is the next step in our time management system that keeps this from happening. That next step is to schedule your tasks. By scheduling, I mean determining how long a task ought to take, and making an appointment with yourself to get it done in a certain block of time. People who don't do this but merely work in order of priority, fall helplessly into the ravenous, salivating jaws of Parkinson's law, which states: "Work expands to fill the amount of time there is to do it."

Parkinson's law is thus one of the deadliest enemies of any organization. It means that tasks will expand up until the deadline for their completion, robbing the organization of other, discretionary work that could be done if the task had been completed efficiently. By scheduling our time, however, we transform Parkinson's law into our most powerful and trusted ally.

I was once asked by the director of a state government agency for "a few tips" on how he could stop working 16-hour days. As I was in the middle of working on a reorganization plan for his agency at the time, I didn't want to take a lot of time to go into this in detail, so I told him I would give him one suggestion that would solve all his problems if he would promise to try it out. He did. The suggestion was to leave his briefcase at the office.

The first night he tried this, he was very nervous, since he had another eight hours worth of work to do that night at home. The next morning, he came flying into the office, grabbed his briefcase, slammed his door and started working furiously to get all those things done that he had been going to do the night before. That evening, he felt much better about leaving his briefcase at the office, and at the end of the week he said "You know, this is amazing. I've not only done everything in eight hours that I used to do in 12 or 16, but to tell you the truth, I think I've gotten more done."

The reason this worked is that if a person allows herself, in the dimmest recesses of her mind to say "If I don't get this done now, I can always take it home and finish it tonight," all that happens is that she has expanded the time there is in which to do the work. And not by a little bit, either. We never say, "I'll do this tonight by 8:00." We just say "tonight." And "tonight" lasts until tomorrow morning. Given this enormous expansion of time, therefore, Parkinson's law takes over, she slows down, and sure enough, she will have to take it home.

Indeed, I think this is the primary cause of office workers' getting behind. They expand the work indefinitely by taking it home to do at night. There being no fixed deadline for when "tonight" ends, they may put it off until late, or they may work on it lethargically. Or something else may come up that causes them to put it off. In any case, there comes a time when there is a stopping point—the time when they finally get too tired to continue. So the task isn't completed. But that's okay, of course, because if they don't catch up tomorrow, they can always take it home and do it tomorrow night.

To put a stop to this inefficient cycle, and to make sure work gets done in the shortest reasonable amount of time, effective workers set their own deadlines. And this is done by scheduling.

Ideally, scheduling is easy to do. There are only two steps. Look at the right side of the form you used to make up your list of things to do. Determine realistically when you start your day (I say realistically, because there is often a great difference between getting to work at 8:00 and starting work at 8:00). The first question then is "What is the most important thing I can do today?" The answer to that question is on the left side of the form—it's whatever A-1 is. Write the A-1 task on the line on the schedule form which corresponds to the time of day you begin work.

The next question is "How long will this take?" Make a reasonable estimate. If the answer is more than 15 minutes, draw a line through the time blocks that will be used by A-1. If the answer is an hour and a half, for example, and you start work at eight, you will have a line from A-1 through the 9:15-9:30 time block.

Next, ask yourself, "What is the next most important thing I can do?" Write the A-2 task on the 9:30 line. Again, estimate how long that will take, and block that time out. Continue this way throughout the day, until the entire day is scheduled.

You now have set near-term deadlines for each task for which there is time. These deadlines are based not on when the task is actually due, but on the amount of time it ought to take to do it. You will thus have Parkinson's law on your side, pushing you to get the task done by the deadline, instead of working against you, causing you to extend the task as described above.

It is hard to overstate the power of working in this way. As alluded to earlier, many workers spend their entire day working on a task that they could complete in two hours if it were due in two hours. The fact that the deadline is distant or vague allows or encourages them to slow down. By setting our own deadlines, we will get the same type of effort at all times as when we have put the task off until the last possible minute, and so we may be able to multiply our productivity by a factor of three or four.

Of course, this is the ideal situation, and most people do not work in an ideal environment. Let's look then at a few of the things that make scheduling difficult and how the time-management system overcomes them.

Precision Management

Controlling the Telephone

The first problem the system must handle is the telephone interruption. The telephone provides a special type of interruption because the interrupter is already sitting on your desk and is armed with a bell which he keeps ringing until you let him take control of your time. Each of these interruptions breaks our train of thought, taking more of our time than the length of the call itself and making it difficult to stick to the daily schedule.

In The Winning Organization, no one is accessible to the telephone unless she wants to be. All calls are screened. When a person desires uninterrupted time to work on an important task, callers are told she is unavailable at the moment and a message is taken. Because people work according to a schedule, however, the caller can also be told approximately when the person will call back, thus avoiding the situation in which calls fly back and forth for days, each person trying to find the other person at an available moment.

For example, a worker might set the time between 11:00 and 12:00 for calls. If you call her at 9:30, when she is working on a top priority, you will be told she is unavailable but will call you back between 11:00 and noon. You don't have to wonder, therefore, when or if she is going to return your call. If you aren't going to be available during those hours, the receptionist will ask you to recommend another time. That time will be put on the message and becomes an exception to the worker's schedule. One or two such exceptions won't materially alter her ability to meet her self-imposed deadlines.

Some organizations, of course, are not large enough to afford to hire a receptionist. In such circumstances, people can take turns being the receptionist for telephone purposes. For example, if the organization has only five people, each can take a day to be the one to answer the phones. That person won't get as much of his own work done that day as usual, of course, but on the other four days of the week he will get so much more accomplished that the temporary setback is more than offset.

In such circumstances, if one of the four or five employees is a secretary, the tendency, born of traditional organizations' role models, is to have the secretary answer the phone all the time. Secretaries also have their train of thought interrupted by phone messages, and organizations who follow this practice frequently find their secretaries, too, can get behind on important work. Taking the secretary off perpetual phone duty can produce amazing increases in his or her productivity.

Earlier, I defined scheduling as an appointment with yourself. The telephone procedures described above work in The Winning Organization, because such appointments are treated as being every bit as important as an appointment with a customer or as important as a two-hour staff meeting during which calls are held. The system works because workers are never so important that they must respond to every phone call immediately. Traditional organizations allow workers' phone messages to be held while they are at lunch or are sick or at conferences or at C priority meetings, during all of which they accomplish absolutely nothing. But when the worker tries to get the important work of the organization done, traditional organizations allow—even encourage—a barrage of interruptions that hinder progress. If those organizations used the same systems they use to cover for workers when they are at lunch to cover for them while they are doing top priority work, they would have the same edge in effectiveness that The Winning Organization enjoys.

Coping with the Unexpected

In traditional organizations, the crisis is another reason why many people are unable to increase their effectiveness by scheduling. Much of what The Winning Organization does to avoid this problem is preventive in nature. Crises don't happen very often because results are clearly defined, responsibilities are clear, and workers' daily plans are connected to an overall, organizational strategic plan. Because the events leading to top priority results are planned, workers are troubled by fewer unexpected events in their efforts to achieve their goals. The kind of daily crisis so often seen in traditional organizations ("We just live from crisis to crisis around here; it's the nature of the job") is therefore not a time management problem for workers in The Winning

Organization. Nonetheless, the unexpected does arise from time to time, and unexpected events are another problem the system must handle.

Unexpected events can be of two types, those that are of high priority and those that are not. In traditional organizations, where purposes are often lost sight of, workers find it hard to distinguish between the two. The fact that the unexpected event is a surprise always makes it seem important, and workers wind up dropping everything to respond to events that, under close scrutiny, may not be as important as the project they leave.

With their goals clear, and with a plan for the month set, workers in The Winning Organization can distinguish between the trivial and the important. Unexpected events that are not related to achievement of top priority goals are therefore not treated as crises but are put off for another day or not dealt with at all.

How top priority, unexpected events are handled depends on how often such surprises occur. If the unexpected, top priority event happens rarely, workers need not worry about it. In the real world, from time to time, the schedule is going to get destroyed completely. The time management system is so powerful, that the worker will quickly recover those lost hours.

On the other hand, if for some reason (more likely to happen in a traditionally structured organization) a top-priority, unexpected event happens regularly, then the rule is "Never be taken by surprise by that which happens every day." Any regularly-occurring demand on your time can be anticipated and taken into account when you schedule.

If you are troubled by frequently occurring unexpected events in your job, ask yourself how much of your time gets chewed up on an average-to-bad day by such occurrences. If the answer to that question, for example, is ninety minutes, schedule "unexpected events" in the last hour and a half of your day.

Of course, crises aren't known for their punctuality. But by scheduling them for the last block of the day, you make it impossible for them to be late. They can only be early. If they are early, you have a choice. You can either drop what you're doing and respond to the crisis now, putting off what you are working on until the afternoon when the crisis had been scheduled. Or, if you have the courage to stare the unexpected in the face, realizing that if you had been out when this happened that it would have managed to keep just fine until you returned, you can put off dealing with it until the last block of your day. Thus, when your boss comes in and says "You won't believe what just happened now," you can look at him cooly and say "I thought that might happen, and I have scheduled time to handle it at 3:30."

Other types of predictable, unexpected events may occur in small doses throughout the day. Clients, for example, may drop in without appointments, expecting and even needing to be seen. In such circumstances, you can follow the same principle of not being taken by surprise by that which happens every day. Since you know they are coming, though not necessarily who or precisely when, you can make appointments for them. Ask yourself how many usually show up and how long they take. Then schedule those appointments at the times you feel they are most likely to appear. If the person is late, you can go on to the next priority, thankful for the opportunity to get ahead of schedule.

If the unexpected person is earlier than you scheduled him, you have a choice. You can either allow him to interrupt you, knowing you can use the time you scheduled for him to catch up later. Or you can have someone tell him you are working on an extremely important project that is due that day (all true–it says so on your schedule) and ask him if he'd mind waiting. When the time comes for his appointment, you can apologize for his having to wait and tell him that if he were to call ahead in the future, he wouldn't have to wait a single minute. The advantage of the last approach is that it teaches people who don't make appointments that they can't just walk in and interrupt you at any time. They take the consequences for not respecting your time and hence learn to call ahead. They thus become less of a time management problem in the future. Obviously, such an approach is best used for those who are recurrent visitors and who are not in dire, life-threatening need (this approach is not recommended for hospital emergency rooms, for example).

The System in Action

The schedule of a person employed in a traditional setting appears on the following page, illustrating many of the points covered so far. She wrote the items on her "to do" list in the order that she thought of them. A-2 and A-3 were both big projects with distant due dates, and she broke them down into components. She elected to finish one component of each that day in order to make regular progress on both. She left time for two unexpected clients, one of whom she expected would be waiting for her when she returned from lunch, since, it seemed to her, that that was "always the case." Since her boss, despite all her efforts to get him to be more respectful of her planning, frequently sprang an assignment on her late in the day, she scheduled that (sometimes, she said, she writes "stupid intrusions from the boss" in her frustration). On this day she elected to make all her calls in the morning. Anyone calling in the afternoon would be told she would return the call the next day. Sometimes, she leaves a half hour in the morning and another half hour in the afternoon for calls.

Near the end of the day, she schedules 15 minutes to go through the paper that has accumulated in her in-box during the day. She does no work on any of this at this point (nothing urgent can come via the mail) but rather makes decisions on what to do with the paper. Trivial paper she throws away. She records small bits of information from other pieces of paper (such as addresses or notes to call someone) and then throws them away. Still others are filed as records or as resources, and some are put in a special file for future action. This "future file" is a series of 31 file folders, each corresponding to a day of the month. Each piece of paper for future action is placed in the folder whose number corresponds to the day she decides to handle it. She refers to the appropriate folder each day in making up her "to do" list.

The last 15 minute block of each day is set aside for planning the next day. During this time she examines her broad goals for the month, analyzes her progress toward achieving her goals, makes a new list of things to do, sets her priorities, and writes her schedule. Looking ahead, we can see that tomorrow she will pro-

TO DO TODAY   SCHEDULE

Priority	To Do		Schedule
B-3	LETTER TO DIAMOND	7	
A-3	PREPARE FOR WORKSHOP (FLYER, NOTES, (SIZE OF GROUP CONFIRMED)		Arrive, coffee, etc.
			A-1 Report to Alice finished
		8	
A-1	REPORT TO ALICE		
B-2	LETTER TO HILTON	9	
C	MEET WITH SARA RE XEROX USE		Unexpected client
A-2	DETERMINE BUDGET ABILITY FOR NEXT YEAR (CLOSURE WITH JANE, FIGURES FROM FRED)		Break
		10	A-2 Get closure on budget for year
			Calls
B-4	INVESTIGATE INSURANCE RAMIFICATIONS FOR PROJECT #3	11	
A-4	MEET WITH MORTON ABOUT NEW CONTRACTS		Lunch, Morton, re further contracts
		12	
B-1	LETTER TO CYNTHIA		
		1	Unexpected client
			A-3 Finish flyer for workshop
		2	
			B-1 Letter to Cynthia
		3	Unexpected assignment from the boss
		4	
			In-box decisions
			Plan tomorrow
		5	
		NIGHT	

bably do more work on what today was A-2 and A-3, that she may have some work left over if the boss's unexpected assignment was larger than usual, and that she will probably get to B-2, 3, and 4. On the other hand, there may be some new A priorities that arise, perhaps from her phone calls, perhaps from the in-box, perhaps from the pieces of paper in the future file folder which corresponds to tomorrow's date. These may cause today's B priorities to be put off further.

There are two primary benefits to employees using this basic system. First, it makes it practically impossible for them to do unimportant work. Things are scheduled too tightly for C priorities to squeeze in. And second, because they are working toward near-term deadlines at all times, they will get the same type of effort at all times as people do when they have put things off until the last possible moment. They are thus working in a more efficient, concentrated fashion on the most important things and are hence as valuable to the organization as it is possible to be.

Chapter 6

Precision Management Controls

In the preceding chapters, we've concerned ourselves with creating an organizational structure that is hospitable to producing results. In the remaining chapters, we will look at the management practices that enable people to take full advantage of that structure.

The role of the manager who uses the Precision Management process is to get results from the people she supervises. Put another way, the manager's job is not to do things directly but to make sure things get done. Or, to put it still another way, the manager's job is to do things that enable others to do the work.

Managers in The Winning Organization get results through others primarily by creating conditions that encourage those others to want to do the work. These inducements are quite different from those offered by other organizations. As discussed previously, people in traditional organizations are offered higher wages, better retirement benefits, more generous medical insurance, longer vacations, company gymnasiums, and other "motivators" that have nothing to do with the nature of the job itself. It is as if management says, "We know this job is demeaning, boring, and a drag on your life, so to make up for it we'll give you all these things to compensate (wages, in fact, are called compensation). When, to management's surprise, the ungrateful workers turn out to be surly, resentful, unreliable, and disloyal, they are given even greater "compensation."

To enjoy such benefits, however, workers must be away from work. They must be sick or retired or on vacation or enjoying their leisure time after work. While the organization's benefits may make this part of their lives much better than ever before, the job itself becomes only more dismal by comparison, thereby encouraging absenteeism and abuse of the generous sick-leave benefits. And, happy as the workers may be when benefits are increased, it will not be long until they again show they are bored or apathetic or hostile with regard to the job.

Workers today have basic needs that are different than those of workers 50 years ago. The traditional organization frustrates workers' abilities to meet those needs in productive ways, driving workers to get satisfaction in ways that hurt the organization. Using Precision Management techniques, managers in The Winning Organization enable workers to get those needs met in ways that produce results for the organization.

In general, Precision Management recognizes that the non-supervisory personnel of an organization are the ones that do the work. Responsibility for that work is therefore given to the workers themselves, rather that to supervisory personnel, and management becomes a source of help to the worker rather than a goad. This not only motivates the worker to top production, but allows management to spend less time worrying about the details of production and more time to think strategically, to concentrate on grasping the opportunities that traditional managers are too mired in the muck of day-to-day details to see.

The first steps in the Precision Management process have been discussed previously. The manager defines the results required by the job and how the worker will be measured. Workers then propose to management the targets they think they can reach. Management either accepts these targets or rejects them, in which case the worker is responsible for developing a new recommendation. Once the target is accepted, management defines the checkpoints, the times at which the worker is to report his progress. The frequency of these checkpoints depends on the complexity of the task and upon the individual manager's anxiety about the outcome or about the worker's performance.

Levels of Control

Once workers are aware of the results they are to achieve and have had their targets approved, managers do one more key thing that insures the quality of the work performed. They define the level of control the individual worker is authorized to exercise in pursuing each result.

These levels of control define how much say the manager and the worker each have in deciding how each result is to be achieved. Essentially, there are four degrees of control:

1. *The Authority for Self-assignment.*

At this first degree of control, the worker has been given or has take the authority to decide for himself what he does. The term "self-assignment" means that the worker is the source of his own assignments; they come from himself, not from others. When a worker is operating at this level, he sees what needs to be done, he does it, and that is the end of it. Many managers are of course justifiably nervous about giving workers this much control because if the worker sees the wrong things that need to be done, there may be some problems in achieving the desired results. There is also a great potential for chaos if everyone a manager supervises is given this much control.

2. *The Authority for Self-assignment Provided Regular Progress Reports Are Received.*

The second degree of control gives the supervisor a bit more insurance that the right things are being done. When a worker is operating at this level, he sees what needs to be done, he does it, but at some point, the frequency of which is determined by the supervisor, he tells the boss what he has done. This gives his supervisor some increased control over what happens because if she doesn't like what he has done, she can see to it that things get fixed. How often these progress reports are received depends on how anxious she is about her employee's performance.

3. *The Authority to Recommend Self-assignment.*

If the supervisor is very anxious about the worker's performance, if, in other words, she is worried that she is going to have to take steps to "fix it" more often than she feels is tolerable either for her or for the organization, then she might want the worker to exercise still less control. When a worker is operating at this third level, he is still the source of his own assignments. In this case, however, he gets approval from the supervisor before he acts. Here the supervisor has still more control because if she doesn't like the recommended course of action, she can stop the person from doing anything before he does it. At this third level, as with level two, workers also provide progress reports once their recommendations are approved.

Just as level two contains gradations of control in the form of varying frequencies of reports, so level three comes in a variety of shades. In some cases, managers might want daily plans from some employees, perhaps in the form of the prioritized list of things to do described in chapter five. More generous portions of control at this level come in the form of plans for the month or plans for the quarter or an overall plan for achieving the target. These gradations depend on the supervisor's degree of anxiety about the employee's performance in pursuing the particular targets.

4. *No Authority for Self-assignment.*

If the boss is not only anxious about the worker's performance but downright psychotic, she might be tempted to allow him still less control, and the only place lower to go is the fourth degree of control. At this level, it doesn't matter whether the worker sees what needs to be done. He just does what he is told to do.

This fourth level of control is rarely used in organizations using Precision Management methods. In the other three levels, the worker has the authority for thinking, for deciding what needs to be done. At level four, that responsibility is transferred up, away from the place where the work is actually done, to the management level. This inevitably produces more work for the manager, as we will see in the next chapter, because whenever someone is unsure what to do next, the manager will be given the assignment, by the worker, to figure that out. The more people the manager supervises, and the more complex their jobs, the more such assignments she will receive every day.

Putting workers at level four produces more serious problems than this, however. For one thing, the workers are the ones with the day-to-day, hands-on experience with the work itself. They know better than anyone else the problems of doing the work, and quite frequently they have some good ideas about opportunities that exist for the organization. Traditional organizations are often oblivious to those problems and slow to recognize those opportunities because the person who is aware of them is not authorized to do the necessary thinking to make sure something gets done about it. Workers in traditional organizations are often heard grumbling about how stupid management is for not seeing something or for not doing things a different way, but management never hears this because workers are discouraged from being involved in this "thinking" aspect of their jobs.

Motivation and Control

The major cost traditional organizations pay when they put people at level four, however, is that the need for control is a very important motivator. When people are denied control over what they do, they are told, in essence, that they are too stupid to figure these things out, that thinking is the province of the smart people, the people who make higher salaries. Workers tend to resent this.

I was giving a speech a while ago to a group that included an airline president. Before the speech, which happened to be on this subject, he said "I'll tell you what you can tell me. What you can tell me is how to deal with these kids today." I asked him what he meant by that, and he said "Aw, these kids today. You know you can't get help like you used to when I was a boy. These kids today have no respect for authority. They're hostile, apathetic, resentful. They even try to sabotage what you do. If you fire one, the next one turns out to be even worse. How do you deal with these kids today?"

Precision Management

During my speech, I described the four degrees of control and asked the group "What happens when you put people at degree of control number four, where they are denied the authority to think for themselves. What are some of the feelings this arouses?" The group responded "They get hostile, resentful, apathetic, they have no respect for your authority, and they even try to sabotage what you do." I looked at the airline president expecting to see a light bulb appear over his head. But he was a dyed-in-the-wool, traditional manager. He stood up. He said "It's the boss's job to tell people what to do" and walked out.

This attitude brings more woe than results to the life of the traditional manager. Most modern workers have a need for control. If they don't get that need met through doing the job, they will get it anyway because it is a primary motivator. Denied control over their actions on the job, people will get this basic need fulfilled by taking control in a different way. One way they will do this is to play a game with the supervisor that people with no control over their lives have been playing and winning ever since slavery was invented. The game is simple—to figure out how to do exactly what the boss said to do but in such a way that everything gets screwed up. Once everything is screwed up, they get to experience the sweet satisfaction of saying "But boss, I just did what you told me to do." And they get even more satisfaction if the boss's boss comes to find out what happened. At which point they can say "Our boss can't communicate with us very well. He tells us to do one thing and then gets mad when we do it. It's awfully hard to work for such an incompetent."

It is important to realize that the workers will always win such a game because no matter how foolproof management's instructions are, the workers are the ones, in the final analysis, that control the doing. And they can do it with dedication and maximum effort, or they can do it lazily, or they can do it looking for ways to screw it up. And no matter how brilliant the original decision was, that decision is only as good as the decision the worker makes as to which of these three approaches he takes to carrying it out.

By no means the worst example of this comes from a small police department. One of the officers had become a little lackadaisical in some of his procedures, and as punishment his Sergeant decided the officer should walk a beat for the day instead of riding around in the patrol car as usual. All the way downtown, the Sergeant complained to the officer about his attitude, and he dumped him off downtown with the words "You walk a beat for eight hours, then we'll talk some more about it!"

A few hours later there was a robbery downtown, and the officer in question was raised on his radio and asked how long it would take him to respond. He said "About an hour, if I run." When asked why it would take so long, he informed the dispatcher that he had been told to walk a beat all day and had been walking for more than two hours now and that it would take him that long to run back.

Was this officer stupid for walking his beat in a straight line from downtown? Or did he show a genius-level intelligence for figuring out how to do what he was told in such a way that everything got screwed up? In any case, he met his needs for control, and his supervisor was admonished by a superior for not giving more clear instructions to the officer.

At level four, then, people have a positive incentive to perform incompetently. It defends their egos to do so; it gives them back the sense of control that they lose when the boss tells them what they can and can't do. By unwittingly giving their people this psychological reward for doing the work poorly, traditional managers have to spend a lot more effort to get good results.

In The Winning Organization, people are put at level four only in three circumstances. The first is when they are in training, since a person who is new to the job may not know the job well enough to recommend what to do. The second instance is in an emergency. And the third instance is in response to reverse delegation, as will be discussed in the next chapter.

Climbing the Control Ladder

The remaining levels of control are a ladder for people to climb. When a person first comes on board, and we are satisfied that he

knows the job well enough to make an intelligent recommendation, we start him at level three. This is also what we do
when the person has been in the job a long time, but we are a new
supervisor. We do this because no matter how good the person
seems to be on paper, we don't know yet whether he is going to
do the right things. And there is only one definition of "the right
things." The right things are the kinds of things we would tell them
to do if we had the time and inclination to do that.

So he begins by bringing us recommendations as to how he is
going to go about achieving the results for which he is responsible. As we accept these or reject these or ask for modifications of
these recommendations, he learns what the right things are.
There's no point bringing us recommendations to do "the wrong
things," i.e. the kinds of things that he may personally think are
swell but at whose mere mention we shudder in horror. There's
no point because he is the one responsible for achieving the results, and if he doesn't bring us a recommendation we can approve, he will keep having to listen to why we don't like his
proposed actions and will keep getting sent back for new recommendations. He won't be able to start on fulfilling the responsibilities on which he is measured until he comes up with an acceptable plan.

After he has learned the kinds of recommendations we approve,
and after he has proven to us over a period of time that he is
capable of seeing the right things to do, we should become more
trustful of him and more comfortable about the quality of his performance. At this time, we may also tire of listening to all these
wonderful recommendations which we always approve.

In any case, once our anxiety goes down, it is time to increase
our effectiveness as managers by giving him more control. We do
this by moving him to level two, by telling him he needn't bother
us anymore with his plan for achieving his results, but we would
like to be kept informed as before.

At first, our anxiety may be such that our checkpoints may be
quite frequent, even as often as once a week, depending on our
degree of anxiety. At those meetings, we will get an accounting of
the things he has been doing. If we find at these meetings that he

has suddenly begun to do "the wrong things," we will put him back at level three, asking for a plan of action. But if, sure enough, he is still doing the kind of things we would have told him to do if we had the time and inclination to do that, then we may eventually be comfortable enough to make the checkpoints less frequent. And eventually, less frequent still.

And finally, maybe, he might get to the point where he can graduate to level one. When an employee is at level one, there are no checkpoints at all. There are no checkpoints because you have approved the target he is trying to achieve, and there is no use in taking his time away from pursuing that objective by bothering him about what he is doing. There is no use because he has proven, over a long enough period for you to be certain, that the things he does are the kinds of things you would tell him to do if you had the time and inclination to do so.

When employees are at level one, management hears from them only if they are having difficulty achieving their targets. Otherwise, management assumes that things are on-target and does not want to be bothered with reports that merely confirm this assumption.

In the unlikely event that you are ever lucky enough to get all your people working at level one on all of their responsibilities, you will be able to spend the time you would otherwise spend in making sure people are doing the right things looking out your window, thinking creative and progressive thoughts, thinking strategically about how to handle the future, seeing where trends are leading and to grasp the opportunities they offer. That's why managers' offices have windows, to keep that goal forever in your mind.

Usually, employees will operate at different levels of control on different responsibilities. For each approved target, management should tell the employee which level of control he has. The way to determine the level of control is to assess your own personal anxiety that the employee will go about achieving the target without mishap. If the anxiety is low, the employee's degree of control can be high. But if you are worried about errors, the employee gets less control so you can make sure the organization achieves the results it requires.

It is also important to stress that it is only at level one that checkpoints are not used and that people get there only when we are absolutely certain that such checkpoints are not necessary. At all other levels, including level four, managers should keep track of employee progress. Even if you have approved an excellent plan, even if you have told an employee precisely what to do, it is better to check periodically to make sure he is making progress toward the target than to wait until the end to be surprised that his performance was different than you expected.

A calendar, on which meetings to review employee progress are recorded, is the easiest, cheapest, and one of the most effective of all management controls. It lets employees know that you are serious about their achievement of their targets. It helps avoid crises and the poor quality of last-minute work by encouraging them to make regular progress toward their targets, instead of putting work off until the due date is excruciatingly near. And it enables the manager to spot problems with an employee's work while there is still a chance for corrective action.

Use of the control scale enables the manager to keep things under control while simultaneously empowering employees. Traditional managers attempt to keep things under control by telling employees what to do or by developing rigid procedures, either of which places the employee at level four on the control scale. Traditional managers thus have to try to get their results from workers who feel belittled and who feel some sense of resentment or apathy as they go about their jobs.

Traditional managers are in this fix in part because they see only two options, they see only levels one and four on the control scale. They see only a choice between controlling things directly or turning people loose to do their own thing, something which would produce chaos. By using the intervening two levels on the control scale, managers using Precision Management techniques gain the motivational advantages of giving their workers a sense of control of their work while also keeping things under control themselves.

All of this is easier to understand in the abstract than it is to apply to concrete, day-to-day situations. On page 112, then, are some hypothetical situations for you to analyze. Although the job described may not be familiar to you, the situation is generic enough to be understood by anyone. Read the four scenarios and answer the questions following. As the questions all relate to the degree of control the employee exercises in the various situations, a summary of the control scale is given below:

---

1. The authority for self-assignment
2. The authority for self-assignment, provided boss is kept advised.
3. The authority to recommend self-assignment
4. No authority for self-assignment.

After you do answer the questions, compare your answers to those in the following discussion.

Control Quiz Discussion

In the first situation, Frank is not exercising any control over what he does. He is at level four on the control scale. This is not the worst kind of level four assignment because it is a creative task. He can decide which clients to spotlight, what words to chose, and so forth, but he has exercised no authority for self-assignment; the assignment has not come from him but from the boss.

To give him some authority for self-assignment, you first have to define the result you want from Frank. Why do you want these stories written? To change people's attitudes toward the agency? Then give him that responsibility, and let him decide how to go about doing it. At degree of control number three, the authority to recommend self- assignment, he would develop a plan for pursuing this objective; once the plan was approved, you would define how to measure progress and negotiate checkpoints for reviewing it. At degree of control number two, the plan would be assumed to be all right, and the only thing you would have to do is to define the measures and negotiate the checkpoints. At level one (very unlikely if Frank had never done public relations work

CONTROL QUIZ

You are the Emergency Services Director of a centralized mental health center. You supervise the directors of three programs and one staff person named Frank. Frank's major responsibility is for securing funding for the three programs, which he does by writing grant proposals to state, local, federal, and private organizations. In his previous job, his primary responsibility was public relations.

1. At a meeting of your staff (the four people you supervise) you mention that your boss is worried about the prevailing negative attitude in the community toward the mental health center. It is his feeling that the community regards the center as being an ineffective body which serves only transients. You tell Frank to write some public interest stories for release to the press which describe the good things the programs do and which spotlight clients who have gone on to play a productive role in the community.

   a) What degree of control is Frank exercising?
   b) What could you do to increase his control?

2. You give Frank total responsibility for the public knowing and valuing the good things emergency services programs do. He prepares a brief proposal, outlining actions he could take. Two of these you approve, one you don't like at all, and two you aren't sure about. You tell Frank you'll get back to him later and put the programs in your briefcase to study that night at home.

   a) When Frank submitted his proposal to you, what degree of control was he exercising?
   b) After you told him you'd get back to him, what degree of control was he exercising?

3. Frank hears that the state may have some funding available to support one of your programs. He calls the state and finds out about it. He sends you a report, spelling out the facts. The last sentence of the report is "Do you think it's worth going after?"

   a) What degree of control is Frank exercising?
   b) What could you do to increase his control?

4. You make it clear to Frank that he has the authority to pursue all reasonable funding for emergency services. He writes a proposal and submits it. Afterwards, he writes you a memo indicating that he has done so and describing the current status of the application.

   a) What degree of control is Frank exercising?
   b) If you wanted to, how would you increase it?

for you before), you would hear from Frank only if he were having difficulty achieving his result.

In situation two, you have given Frank responsibility for a result. You seem to have put him at level three, because that is the degree of control he is exercising when he brings you his plan. But once you say you have to think this over, you have put him back to level four.

Many people find this situation difficult to understand, so let's go into it a bit more. If you are going to think the proposals over because you are unsure of them, it means you are taking the authority for thinking away from Frank. It also means that you are going to do some work on the proposals yourself. If you take them home and think about them, revise a few thoughts, clarify a few options, maybe make a few calls to get information not contained in the proposals, you will be ruining your personal life in order to do work for one of your subordinates. And after burning the midnight oil (while Frank goes out and has a good time), you will present Frank with the results of this work. At this stage, the only way that Frank can prove that you were wrong to screw up his brilliant ideas is to carry them out poorly. And when someone (your boss perhaps) complains to Frank about the lack of progress, he can turn around and say "It's not my fault. I gave the boss a brilliant proposal, and he told me to do this instead. Do you see what we have to put up with down here?"

So what do you do if you are unsure whether an idea is a good one or not? If you are unsure, tell Frank that. Try to tell him why you are unsure, what additional information you'd like to have, what points you are uneasy about. Then give him the assignment of thinking it over. Give him the assignment to gather the information, clarify the points, or explore the ramifications. Give him the assignment to do the thinking and to come back to you with a new proposal which you can approve. Then, when he begins to work on the project, all actions he takes are actions he recommended, actions he decided were the right ones (and which you approved). This means that the only way he can prove he was right is to put everything he has into making sure this works. It's his plan. He owns it. His ego is on the line (though he does have the security, at level three, that you thought it was a good idea too).

The first instance is the traditional way of managing. It results in you getting overworked and running the risk of getting indifferent effort and results from your employees. In the second instance, you employ Precision Management methods. By doing so you work fewer hours and get better effort and results from your people.

In situation three, Frank is almost at level two. But in the last sentence he throws it away and puts himself at level four by asking to be told what to do.

In situation two, we saw how easy it was for the boss to put an employee at level four without meaning to. In situation three we see how easy it is for employees to put themselves at level four without meaning to. In asking management to make this decision, the employee abdicated his authority for self-assignment and, in the process, gives an assignment to the boss to do the work of reading the memo, grasping its implications, maybe asking a few questions to clarify some points, and coming up with a recommendation. To increase Frank's control from this abysmal level, you need to ask him to finish his work. "Frank, your job is not to ask me questions like this but to bring me recommendations to approve or disapprove. In order to make the decision you've asked me to make here, I need to know if you think it's worth going after and why."

In situation four, Frank is exercising degree of control number two—the authority for self-assignment provided the boss is kept informed. He has decided to submit a proposal, and he is keeping you informed as to his activities in pursuing his responsibilities for getting funding for the agency. If you had worked with Frank for many years and had no anxiety about his performance, you could increase his control by telling him you no longer need progress reports from him. You assume he will be working successfully toward his targets and don't want him to take time away from that to tell you that things are going the way you think they are. You do, however, expect to be told if Frank is having difficulty.

In making the decision to put Frank at level one on the control scale, you must make sure that he sees this as a compliment, that he sees it as a rare reward for someone who is so capable. You also have to take special care to give Frank regular doses of recognition for being such a rare individual.

The Right Level of Control

As indicated previously, the main barometer for deciding whether an employee should have his control increased is the degree of anxiety the boss feels about the task. To some degree, this depends on the individual manager. Some are more nervous than others, and it takes their employees longer to rise on the control scale. As a result of these differences, there are no absolutely right or wrong answers to the following questions, but see how close you come to my answers:

1. At what level of control would you put an old hand who has been with you for years and who you trust implicitly?
2. At what level of control would you put an old hand who has been with you for years but with whom you have a history of disagreement and conflict?
3. At what level would you put a new employee, fresh from a brilliant college career?
4. At what level would you put a person who has brought you brilliant recommendations over the last six months and carried them out well?
5. At what level would you put a new employee who has 20 years of experience in a similar job for another employer?
6. At what level would you put a group of employees with six to ten years of experience in their present jobs if you were their new boss?
7. At what level would you put an old hand, who you trust implicitly and who is working on a project that may spell success or failure for your organization and your career, depending on the outcome?

Now the answers:

In the first instance, you would certainly put this person at least at level two, and the progress reports would probably be relatively infrequent. If you truly trust him implicitly, if you are sure that what he will do is exactly the kind of thing you would tell him to do if you had the time and inclination to do so, you would put him at level one.

In the second situation, the person should be at level three. Even though he has been with you a long time, he has not learned what kinds of things you want done. You need to review his recommended self-assignments before you let him take any action.

In the third instance, I would put the person at the most remedial level of level three, reviewing her daily self-assignments on the time-management form described in the previous chapter. Regardless of how intelligent and knowledgable her college experience showed her to be, she still does not know the things that enable her to exercise more control; she still does not know your values and standards and the kinds of things you want done in certain situations.

As to question four, it may be time to move this person from level three to level two. The progress reports would probably be relatively frequent—perhaps weekly—as you assure yourself that he indeed was ready for this increased authority.

The answer to question five is similar to that to question three. The person's track record for another boss does not entitle her to greater control than any other new person. The authority for self-assignment is increased only when employees learn the kinds of things you want them to do. So this person should also be at level three.

Similarly, then, if you are the new boss in question six, all employees start at level three. They are all experienced, but they don't yet know the kinds of things you want done. They may have all done exactly what their old boss wanted, but you may well have very different standards than she has. What she wanted done may strike you as the wrong things. Although their experience may enable some of them to rise fairly rapidly on the control scale, nonetheless, all the employees in question six start with the authority to recommend self-assignment.

In situation seven, your normal degree of confidence and trust for the employee may be tempered by your overriding anxiety about the outcome of this particular task. Since the employee's authority is directly related to only one variable, and since that variable is your level of anxiety about his or her performance, you would probably put this old hand either at level three or at a very low level of level two (frequent progress reports).

This Precision Management method of keeping things under control while simultaneously empowering the employees works only if they have clear results to achieve. Asking for a recommendation when there are no such clear results turns the authority for self-assignment into a guessing game. An employee needs responsibility before authority makes sense.

Precision Management Questions

Managers using Precision Management methods keep things under control while empowering employees in another way. They know that while staff and workers need to know the right answers, the manager's role is fundamentally different and in some sense the opposite. In order to control while empowering, the manager needs to know the right questions.

Traditional supervisors think they should have all the answers. Whenever they interact with a subordinate, they feel that if they can't answer all the questions and have instant solutions for all the problems, they are failing. Insecure traditional managers either make something up or make a snap decision when they are presented with a problem they really don't have an instant answer for. Or they tell the subordinate they will get back to him later.

The root of this behavior is the traditional manager's concern that the subordinates should have confidence in her and should respect her. By contrast, Precision Management is most concerned that workers should have confidence in themselves.

An employee whose supervisor has all the answers develops a sense of dependency on his boss. He therefore does not grow in his own capabilities. Further, since such managers often think it is their job to tell their employees what to do and how to do it, they tend to foster employee apathy and resentment, as described in the discussion of control. Employees in such circumstances tend to stagnate and decay, making it increasingly difficult for the supervisor to get results.

Precision Management stresses the importance of the manager using questions in interactions with employees. Questions empower employees while leaving the questioner very much in control. The use of questions is thus another way managers can empower while controlling. For each of the major management functions—planning, enabling, and evaluating—there are several key questions.

The first set of management questions relate to planning. Planning is something managers should never do alone; they should always involve the people who will be carrying out the plan. As will be explored further in Chapter 12, planning departments or staff assigned to planning are extravagances in which The Winning Organization does not indulge, principally because plans made by those who must implement the plan are based on more practical information and are pursued with more enthusiasm.

Sitting down with the people who will implement the plan, the manager facilitates the planning process by asking questions such as:

—What is our purpose?
—What new developments affect us?
—What are the trends?
—How can we take advantage of those trends and develop-
   ments?
—What are the alternatives?
—What problems do you see?
—What opportunities do you see?

In groups larger than six or seven, the manager will find it easier to increase active participation by having small groups of employees meet to discuss each question and then report the results of their deliberations to the large group.

With the data generated in response to these questions, the manager brings the group to focus with questions such as:

—Based on all this, what should we be trying to
   accomplish?

—What should our goals be for the upcoming period?

In all of this, the manager need not play a purely facilitative role. She may have very strong opinions of her own concerning these questions. The manager should always sound out the group first, however. She should question them first, suggest second, and only third state her own opinion. Again, the idea is to empower the employees by making the ideas theirs, where possible, but the idea is also to stay in control and to set the most effective goals for the organization.

Once the goals are set by the planning group, one very powerful next move is to refer to each goal and ask "Who will take responsibility for this?" Again, the manager may have particular people in mind to do certain tasks and can certainly exercise her prerogative to assign responsibility. But where it is appropriate, asking for voluntary assumption of responsibility empowers the group and leads to more committed pursuit of the organization's objectives.

Other planning questions are appropriate after goals have been set and responsibility has been assigned or taken. At meetings with the responsible individual or team these questions can be asked:

—When can you have your plan to me?
—What is your target?
—How will we measure your success?
—What is your timetable?

At such meetings, enabling questions may also be appropriate. Perhaps the most powerful of the enabling questions is "Can you handle this responsibility?" Such a question challenges the employee and encourages self-reliance. In addition to being a good question when it comes to fixing responsibility for achieving part of the organization's planned results, it is an especially useful question to ask when delegating responsibility for a result, as in "John, I would like you to take responsibility for increasing our word-processing productivity through the purchase of new software. Can you handle it?"

This question may be followed up with "How will you go about it?" and/or "When can I see your plan?"

Other important enabling questions can be used in counseling and coaching employees on job performance and motivational issues. These include:
- —How do you feel about your job?
- —What are your frustrations?
- —How much ownership do you feel in your job?
- —Do you know what you want to achieve in your job?
- —What do you need to do your job better?
- —Would you like some increased responsibility?

Other questions enable the manager to help her employees see the connection between doing a good job and growing in their careers. By showing the employee that she would like to help him succeed not only in the job but in his career as well, the effective manager doubles the employee's motivation. These questions include:
- —Do you know what you want to achieve in your career?
- —How can I make your job a means of achieving your career goals?
- —How can I help you build a track-record of excellent performance that will further your career?

Earlier, I stressed the importance of the manager establishing checkpoints at which an employee's performance is reviewed (unless he is at level one on the control scale). At these review meetings, it is again important for the manager to have the right questions. These evaluating questions include:
- —How would you describe your performance?
- —Are you on-target or off?
- —What happened?
- —What went wrong?
- —Why did you do so well?
- —If you had it to do over again, what would you do differently?
- —What can you learn from your experience?
- —How will you do better in the future?
- —If you were going to advise another person who was about to try to achieve this same target, what would you tell him?

These questions help the employee to analyze his experience in trying to reach his targets. They also firmly establish that he is responsible for that performance, not his boss.

As will be explored in more detail in chapter eight, these questions help the employee learn from that experience so he can do better in the future. This is true whether the employee is doing well or poorly. An effective manager wants her employees to be constantly improving because if they are growing in their abilities, the manager will get better and better results from them.

Other evaluating questions should be asked of the whole unit at least once a year to make sure the organization stays as effective as possible. These powerful questions include:

—What are some better ways of doing what we do?
—How can we work smarter?
—How can we make what we do obsolete?

These evaluating questions lead naturally into a new round of planning questions.

It is important to remember that the types of questions we are talking about empower the employee. They tell him that we have confidence in his ability to think, to take responsibility, to be accountable. They treat the employee as an adult and increase his feelings of autonomy, equality, and self-worth. Other types of questions, while also establishing that the questioner is in control, belittle the employee. "Do you really expect to get paid for this?" or "Just how long did you think you were going to be able to keep this job?" are indeed questions, but they are not the kinds of questions an effective manager uses; she wants her people to feel strong as they do the work of the organization, not diminished, angry, or afraid.

By meeting the employee's needs for control while simultaneously keeping things under control themselves, managers in The Winning Organization tap a powerful motivator and direct it toward achieving the right results. At the same time, they are able to turn their attention outward, toward the strategic environment in which the organization finds itself. Unlike traditional managers, they give people control of the "how" of their jobs and are not swamped in the details of their subordinates' performance. As a

Precision Management

consequence, they are not taken by surprise by future events, as are traditional managers; they are able to anticipate and use those events to their advantage.

Chapter 7

Delegating for Results

The most basic features of the Precision Management process are to structure an employee's job so he has responsibility for a result, and to give that employee control of the process of achieving that result while keeping things under control ourselves. This is all we would need to concern ourselves with in an ideal universe where everything went according to plan. But in the real world, we frequently want employees to be responsible for new tasks and duties that crop up in response to changing situations and opportunities. These responsibilities are not part of the employee's job description per se but are one-time, often short-term duties that need to be taken on. The art of giving employees these additional responsibilities is called delegation.

Delegation is the crux of the management process. Our job as managers is to achieve results through others, and to fulfill this role, delegation is a primary tool. Delegation is also a tool managers can use to keep from getting swamped in details so they can keep their eyes on the horizon.

The Reluctance to Delegate

Many managers, however, are reluctant to delegate. When asked why, they cite many reasons, but the major barriers to delegation have their roots in one of three causes. The first is a misunderstanding of the manager's job. Many managers think that the manager's role is to be the best at doing the work, and so they take on many responsibilities that others could assume because they think these are the manager's job. They think employees will have more confidence in them as leaders if they can do the job better than their people can. Related to this is the feeling that "I can do it better and faster." If you see your role, instead, as making sure others get things done, it is easier to delegate. Here your ability to do things better and faster is of no use unless you can transmit those skills to your people, and delegating is one of the ways in which you can help others learn, grow, and develop.

The second cause of not delegating is that managers often delegate the wrong things, and as a result they find that delegation does not significantly reduce their burdens or contribute to the success of the organization. They also sometimes find that employees resent delegation in these circumstances.

The third and most fundamental source of problems in delegating is the almost universal confusion of delegation with telling people what to do. As we saw in the previous chapter, when managers take away people's control by telling them exactly what to do, employees become hostile or, at best, apathetic. In the remainder of this chapter, we will look at how we can eliminate these barriers to delegation.

Lets's begin our discussion by examining what to delegate. As we will see, what you decide to delegate makes an enormous difference in your effectiveness.

Rules of Delegating

The first rule of delegating is: delegate non-management tasks first.

Each supervisor's job can be divided into two parts, the management tasks and the operating tasks. Operating tasks are those in which she achieves results directly. These tasks directly involve the supervisor in doing the work of the organization. Management tasks are those which enable a supervisor to get results through others and are traditionally categorized as planning, organizing, controlling, and evaluating.

As we have seen, however, when managers employ Precision Management methods, the employees themselves take on responsibility for some of these activities. A list of management functions in such an organization is included on the following page.

THE MANAGER'S JOB

Purpose: To accomplish planned results through others.

PLANNING
> Define the mission of the unit
> Define the results necessary to achieve the mission
> Define the budget available to achieve the results
> Facilitate employee determination of how to achieve results
> Set standards and conditions of employment

ORGANIZING
> Determine reporting relationships
> Define jobs of employees (who is responsible for what results)
> Determine the makeup and mission of task forces

ENABLING
> Staff (hire, fire, assign people to jobs)
> Delegate results to employees
> Train employees in skills necessary to achieve results
> Counsel employees in overcoming problems
> Coach employees in how to achieve results as they ask for such assistance
> Recognize and reward employees for achieving results
> Resolve human relations problems among employees
> Make sure employees' motivational needs are being met by the job
> Make sure employees have the information necessary to achieve their results
> Build employee's self image

EVALUATING
> Establish a reporting system
> Review employee progress toward results
> Decide on corrective action

Precision Management

These functions are the manager's first responsibility. A manager is not hired because we need another person to do the work directly; we can hire non-managers to do that. So when managers look at their lists of things to do and try to decide which should be delegated, the first thing they should do is to sort out the management tasks.

Imagine, for example, that the list of tasks below is your list of things to do for tomorrow. There are far too many things here for you to accomplish by yourself in a normal work day, so you want to delegate some of them. Go through the list and decide which are the management tasks and which are the operating tasks. The idea here is not to ask whether a manager should do the task. A manager might well do all of these things. The idea is to ask "If a manager were to do this, would she be managing, or would she be doing the work directly?"

1. Meeting with a subordinate to review her accomplishments during the previous quarter.
2. Doing technical research in order to give a staff person clear instructions.
3. Meeting with subordinates to set goals for next year.
4. Getting the facts necessary to solve a job-related problem brought to you by one of your subordinates.
5. Assigning a person an area of responsibility.
6. Meeting with two subordinates to try to resolve a conflict between them.
7. Going to a trade fair to learn what new equipment is available this year.
8. Dictating a letter to an important client.
9. Writing part of a proposal to get additional funding.
10. Giving a person a raise.
11. Making a formal presentation to a customer, hoping for additional business.
12. Doing research to find out what went wrong.
13. Showing a subordinate how to do a task.
14. Signing employee paychecks.
15. Proofreading a report typed by your secretary.

Now the answers:

1. This is clearly a management function. It is part of your evaluating and motivating responsibilities, and it is an activity which should, if done properly, lead to the growth of the employee.

2. Although the task is being done in order to give the employee direction, this task itself is doing. Here we see an advantage of the Precision Management approach. Using traditional management methods, you are forced to do this task since you must tell everyone exactly what to do. Managers using Precision Management methods don't tell people what to do, they tell them what to accomplish. It is up to the employees to figure out how to do it, so they would, in this instance, be the ones to carry out this non-management task.

3. Here again we have a managing responsibility. This is part of your planning function. The fact that you are involving your subordinates in the process does not make it any less a fulfillment of your planning responsibility.

4. This is doing. And it is an example of reverse delegation, which we will discuss later in this chapter. You are doing a research task for one of your subordinates. Which of you is in charge here?

5. Managing.

6. This is managing. By resolving this conflict, you will enable your subordinates to work together better, or to work separately with less distraction.

7. Doing. Your are finding out an important matter directly, not achieving a result through others.

8. Doing again. Even though there may be compelling reasons for you to do this yourself, you are not managing while you are engaged in this operation.

9. Doing. Fund-raising and writing are both direct work.

10. This could conceivably be a motivating experience for the person, and the decision to do this might have been part of your responsibilities for rewarding and recognizing top performers. In a Precision Management system, this activity would therefore be a management task. But if the case is that you are merely informing

the person that he has indeed stuck it out for another 12 months and that as a result he is getting his automatic 2.7 percent increase, this is not managing. It is a clerical function.

11. Again, this may be an effective use of your time, but it is not a fulfillment of your management responsibilities. Your making the presentation yourself may enhance your chances for success because it makes the customer feel important. But you are achieving the results directly, not through others.

12. Doing the work directly. Once the reasons for the error are discovered, the decision to be made is a management function. But finding the facts is not.

13. Managing. This is training.

14. Doing. Traditional managers of small organizations may do this, and when they do it they may think they are exercising a management prerogative. But this is a task related to fiscal control, a task that accomplishes something directly. Again, under some circumstances, it may be legitimate for a manager to do this, but while he is doing so, he isn't managing his organization.

15. Doing again. And reverse delegation again. Since when did you become your secretary's assistant copy editor? In Precision Management practice, the secretary has full responsibility for the report going out with no errors and does her own proofreading.

The traditional executive, looking at this list, would tend to place first priority on the "doing" functions, leaving the management tasks until there is time. After all, the management tasks don't seem as urgent: Reviewing accomplishments? Those accomplishments aren't going to go away; I can do that as well tomorrow as I can today. Setting goals? Well, we never had goals before, let's not lose our nerve now. Assigning a person an area of responsibility? They'll only screw it up anyhow. And so on. The non-management tasks, on the other hand, are where the action is. They relate directly to the organization's reason for existence. It is thus relatively easy to put the management tasks off, thereby reducing today's workload by about one-third.

In doing so, however, the manager avoids the primary things she is being paid to do, the tasks that distinguish her job from the jobs of the people she supervises. Although her job does include many non-management tasks in which she achieves results directly, her primary job is management. Her primary job is not to do things but to make sure things get done. By others. And in neglecting her management tasks, she avoids the very things that enable those others to get results, thereby hampering her own effectiveness as a manager.

Such a manager is caught, unwittingly, in a vicious circle. The more she ignores the planning and training and motivating and organizing that enable her people to do the work, the less able her people will be to do the job well. The less able her people are, the more direct work she will have to take on. The more direct work she takes on, the less time she will have for the management tasks. Because her people are under-effective, she is continually overworked. No matter how good she is at doing the work herself, she will never be as effective as the manager whose first priority is making the people she supervises as good as or better than she is at doing things.

The effective manager therefore takes the opposite approach to the list of things to do. She normally puts first priority on the management tasks. Even though these may be a small portion of the things she has to do, they are the reason she is a supervisor; they are the most important part of the job. By making this choice, she finds, in the long run, that she has less direct work to do because she takes the time to do the things to develop her people's abilities, to make sure that they know clearly what they are supposed to accomplish, and to make sure they have adequate control over their responsibilities and are motivated to carry them out. By putting her first priority on the one-third of her tasks which are management responsibilities, she makes sure her people are as effective as possible, and she still has time left over for some of the doing tasks.

What happens to the highly important doing tasks which she doesn't have time to get to? Here is the answer I once heard a top executive give: "Put off the things that aren't urgent, and delegate the things that are." While this may be an oversimplification, I think it is a good motto to keep in mind. Your primary job, after all, is not to do things. And if you get swamped in the doing of things, you will not have time for the strategic thinking a manager must do to keep from being ever taken by surprise by new developments.

This choice of which set of activities to put first is somewhat subtle but absolutely fundamental. It is a choice between being swamped and ineffective or being in control while your people achieve ever-better results.

The second rule of delegating is to delegate only top priority tasks. Many managers fail here. Confronted by stacks of trivial items, they parcel them out to their people with the request to "please handle." Because this junk comes from the boss, people tend to give it a higher priority than they should. Though they may recognize it as intrinsically less worthwhile than things they would otherwise do, and though they may be frustrated by this situation, they nonetheless feel that they must put a high priority on it because the boss has indicated she wants the task done. As a result, their energies are wasted on items of low priority while high priority work goes unpursued.

Again, this practice stems from managers not understanding their role. They fail to recognize that their job is to get results from others, and so they clog their people's calendars with items of low importance. As a consequence, their people have less time for high-impact tasks, and the manager's overall effectiveness is reduced.

As explained in chapter five, low-priority work should either be ignored or done only when all high priority work is finished. Managers should put off low-impact work rather than delegate it. If it ever is completed at all, the manager does it when there is time to do it.

Effective managers realize that they must have their people working at all times on tasks which produce high-impact results. They delegate only high-priority work and train their people to set their priorities based on impact. The organization thus gets more important work done and pays for less time that is spent on useful but not very important tasks.

The third and most important rule of delegating is to delegate results not activities.

Delegating is not the same as telling people what to do. When the boss tells her people what to do, she runs into the resistance, apathy, and resentment that managers always reap when they put their people at level four on the control scale (no authority for self-assignment). Then, with the job done poorly, she laments that "if you want it done right, you have to do it yourself."

The effective manager avoids this trap by defining the result she wants from the task and delegating the whole responsibility to a person or a team. She then defines the degree of control the person is authorized to exercise in pursuit of that particular result.

To illustrate, lets look at the hypothetical list of things to do we analyzed earlier. One of the most time-consuming items on that list was number seven, going to a trade fair to learn what new equipment is available this year. The traditional boss would delegate this task by simply telling a person to do it. Then she will worry about whether the employee will see the right things and bring back the right information. Because the employee has this sprung on him, because it may have destroyed his own plans for the day, because he has no control over his actions here, he may greet this assignment as an imposition and pursue it with an attitude that is at best apathetic. Also, since no result has been specified, it is hard for the employee to make intelligent judgments about what information to bring back. And so, as he lackadaisically goes through the exhibits, he doesn't see the right things, and he doesn't bring back the right information.

The effective manager avoids this by first determining why she wants to go to the trade fair to learn about new equipment. After a little analysis, she realizes that she isn't doing it merely to expand her knowledge of this arcane subject. Rather, she has a purpose. It might be phrased as something like "to improve our efficiency." So she calls her employee in and instead of telling him what to do, she gives him some responsibility. She says something like "James, I would like to give you the responsibility, if you will agree to accept it, for improving our efficiency around here through the purchase of new equipment."

This assignment is much more interesting than merely going to the trade fair. It is something James can get his teeth into. It is a project of his own, and it means he's going to have to do a lot of things. And since it is his total responsibility, he will pursue it with more motivation than if he were just doing one activity which was part of an unknown whole.

Of course, the manager does more than merely giving him the responsibility. She also tells him what "improved efficiency" means (a purchase that will more than pay for itself in two years, for example), and she will tell him what the budget constraints are, and she will tell him everything she knows about the subject already, including the fact that there is a trade fair in town this week. But she will not tell him what to do. That is up to him to decide. Unlike the traditional manager who is locked into having him go do one activity, the effective manager, once she has defined the desired result, no longer cares whether he goes to the trade fair or not. She only cares that he achieves the result.

Before he leaves, however, she will also define for him the level of control he is to have in pursuing this responsibility. If she is anxious about how he will go about pursuing his goal, she will put him at level three, in which case he will propose a time at which he will present his plan for achieving the result. If, at that second meeting, she approves the recommendation, they will then set up a series of meetings to review progress. If she is more confident about his ability, she will put him at level two, in which case, before he leaves the first meeting, they will set up a series of checkpoints for progress reports. And if she is absolutely certain that he is going to do exactly the kind of thing she would tell him to do if she had the time and inclination to do so, she will put him at level one, in which case she will hear from him only if he is having difficulty.

By delegating in this way, she not only delegates the task of going to the trade fair, but she simultaneously delegates all related tasks on future days' lists, tasks traditional managers might delegate to different staff people. And she also simultaneously delegates the task of assembling the information gathered from the various investigations. The traditional manager must do this co-ordination herself when she delegates the individual activities to several subordinates. As a result, the effective manager works fewer hours than the traditional manager and, because the workers are more motivated, gets better results.

Managers who do not operate in this highly-effective style, not only fail to give their employees something rewarding to do but tend to attract a lot of the work back to themselves in the form of reverse delegation. Reverse delegation is a burden traditional managers inescapably shoulder when they delegate and manage by putting their employees at level four on the control scale.

Avoiding Reverse Delegation

Reverse delegation, to define it succinctly, is the work you find yourself doing that is related to a responsibility of one of your subordinates. It usually happens after you meet with a subordinate about his work and find that the next move is yours. When the next move is yours, it means you will be "doing" rather than managing. And when the next move is yours it means he will be waiting (perhaps looking out the window) rather than doing. The roles, in short, become reversed.

Reverse delegation is inescapable when work is delegated at level four, when he is merely told what to do. At level four, the worker has no authority to think, to decide what to do. And therefore whenever he is unsure what to do or whenever a problem arises, you will be given the assignment, by him, of figuring that out. And the more people you supervise at level four, and the more fragmented their responsibilities, the more such assignments you will get from them each day.

To dramatize this, let's imagine that I am a typical, traditional, overworked manager. I supervise only four people, but by the end of the day each of them has met with me at least once, and after each meeting I have something I have to do related to the things they were working on. In other words, each of them has managed to give me an assignment.

For a while, I managed to keep up with them by working nights, weekends, and while going to the bathroom, but eventually, I got swamped. A few weeks ago, I picked up Rick Lynch's book, *Precision Management,* and, not having time to read the whole thing, I read the chapter on time management. I tried out the techniques described in that chapter, and by golly, it worked great. It got me to the point where I could get through three or four of those assignments from my people in a single day. But by the end of the day, they had managed to give me four or five more.

Each day, I went to work, made up a list of things to do, I prioritized it, I scheduled uninterrupted time, and then I barricaded my door, praying "Please Lord, don't let anyone come in here with a problem for me today. Let me make some headway, for a change."

Meanwhile, they sat around and complained. "Boy it sure takes him a long time to make a decision. I gave him that problem two days ago, and he still hasn't told me what to do about it yet."

"Well, you think that's bad. I asked him a simple question two weeks ago. He's so embarrassed he hasn't got an answer for me yet that when he sees me coming down the hall, he runs into the bathroom and locks the door."

"Well, at least you've caught a glimpse of him. I've been waiting for a decision for over a month now. Can you believe how mediocrity sinks to the top around here?"

"When is he going to start earning his money?"

"Just another example of the Peter Principle at work."

Then one day, in a flash of inspiration, I realized that my problem wasn't misplaced priorities. My problem wasn't that I was working inefficiently. My problem was that I was working efficiently on top-priority things that I shouldn't be doing in the first place.

So today, things are going to be different. Today, whenever I have a meeting with one of my people about his or her work, I'm going to make sure they aren't left waiting around for a decision. Today, I'm going to give them what they've always dreamed of: instant, decisive action. And today, my door will be open.

So with some trepidation, I open my door. And there, standing in the doorway is the person who is always standing in the doorway when I open my door. It's Bud. And Bud says to me what Bud always says when I see him. He says "Boy, boss, have we got a problem."

As usual, I listen to Bud describe this problem in agonizing detail. It concerns a task I asked him to do last week. He has hit a snag, and is unsure what to do next. He is unsure of our policy on this matter because two of the policies seem to contradict each other in this case.

If I act in my old, traditional way, I will take the assignment from him of figuring out what to do about this problem. This keeps him at level four.

My motives in doing so may be that I don't trust Bud's judgment. Or it may be that I like to feel needed by my people. I may be more concerned that they have confidence in me than they do in themselves. Or it may just be that I don't recognize what Bud is doing to me here; he is putting himself at level four and I may just mindlessly fall into this game.

In any case, by accepting this assignment, I weaken Bud's ability, my own ability to manage, and hence my boss's ability to get results from me. I weaken Bud's ability because whatever abilities he might develop do not develop if I take over his job for him every time he gets stuck. In fact, whatever abilities he once possessed have no doubt decayed during his years of my doing all his thinking for him. I weaken my ability to manage because I am spending time doing Bud's job instead of attending to the management duties mentioned earlier. The whole organization suffers as a consequence.

Traditional managers might disagree with the assertion that I am doing part of Bud's job whenever I solve a problem related to his completing his assignment. They might especially object, as in this case, because this is a policy issue, and I should attend to it as part of my managerial prerogative. That is indeed what Bud might say. And when traditional managers delegate only one activity related to a given result, with some other subordinates doing other activities and they themselves doing others, it is hard to make this distinction. But if I use the Precision Management approach to delegating and give Bud a whole project that is his to be responsible for, it is easier to see that problems that arise relating to completing the assignment are his problems. They are mine only in the sense that they indicate that Bud has insufficient skill or information to achieve the results I am trying to get through him. With this understood, it is clear that my role in a matter such as this is to make sure that Bud acquires the skill or information necessary to fulfill his responsibility, not to do the work myself.

What I want to do, then, is get out of the role of acting as Bud's assistant. I want to stop doing Bud's thinking for him. If I have a high degree of anxiety about his thinking, it is an indicator that I have not been doing a very good job of fulfilling my management responsibility of developing Bud's abilities. I need to start now to remedy this.

Assuming I have indeed given Bud responsibility for a result, I may start by saying "Bud, I want to help you solve this problem. What do you need to know that you don't know now?" To which he replies that he needs to know which of the conflicting policies applies in this case. I say "Bud, if I knew, I would tell you, but I don't. Who else do you think might know?"

"I guess you might call Personnel."

"That sounds like a good place to start." I reach for my pad that says "From the Desk of Richard Lynch" on it and write "Please train Bud in the relative priorities of company policy related to the project for which he is responsible." I sign my name and hand it to him. "If they don't know the answer, ask them who to check with next."

"But that's your job," he complains. It's amazing how often traditional managers hear this statement from their people. In every management text ever written it says that part of the manager's responsibility is to define the jobs of his subordinates. You can always tell when reverse delegation is the rule and who is really in charge; they are the ones who are defining the jobs of others with statements such as "that's her job; that's not my job; that's your job" and so on.

So I may have to do a little training of Bud here. I say "No, Bud, my job is to make sure you have the information and skills necessary to succeed in your job. Since I don't know the answer to this question myself, I am smoothing the way for you to get the information from someone else. By the way, please let me know what you find out, and bring me a recommendation as to what this means you will do next on your project."

"What if I can't find anyone who knows?"

"It's entirely possible that nobody around here knows. If that seems to be the case, I would like you to bring me your analysis of the pro's and con's of following each of the two policies and a recommendation as to which would be the most effective one to follow in your case."

Bud says "But boss. This is part of your job."

"Bud," I say. "Can you handle this?"

As indicated in the last chapter, this is a very powerful question. If Bud says no, says he is incapable of finding out such information, he is admitting to the most abject incompetence. A person who is incapable of finding out such information from internal sources surely can't be capable of doing the rest of his job either. Perhaps sensing this, Bud says "Well, yeah. I could handle it."

"Good." I say. "I thought so."

"But isn't this your job to find out about policy and tell me what to do?"

Obviously, Bud has a poor understanding of my role and of the proper management relationship. In response, I ought to explain our various roles to him in a calm, supportive way. In this case, however, I am losing my patience. I say "Bud, which of us is the boss here?"

"Well, you are. That's why . . . "

"And does this mean you tell me what to do or that I tell you what to do?"

"You tell me what to do. That's why I'm here."

"Well first of all, Bud, it sounds to me an awful lot like you are trying to give me an assignment. And second, I just did tell you what to do: Bring me your analysis of the facts and your recommendation. And third, it is not my job to find out about policy, it is my job to make sure you know about policy. And it is my job to make decisions. When I make the decision about what you should do next on your project, one of the factors I will consider is your analysis of the facts and your recommendation. Make it the best one you can."

We may argue a bit more in this way, as Bud learns what his proper role is in his relationship with me. But when he leaves my office, it is essential to his control and to mine, that he is going to have the authority to do the thinking necessary to succeed in his job. Since I am nervous about the quality of that thinking, I want to review it before he acts on it. I want him firmly at level three on the control scale. But I do want him to have the authority to do all the things necessary to carry out the responsibility I delegated.

In this way, I allow Bud maximum responsibility and control, while keeping things under control myself. As he, and the others, get used to this, they will stop bringing me unfinished work for me to complete. They will stop bringing me, for example, rough drafts instead of finished copies of things. They will learn there is no point saying "We've got a problem" because they know they will be sent out to find a solution to it. They will just say "Boss, we have a problem; here's why we have it; here's the alternatives; and here's my recommendation. They will be converted into a source of ideas, in the form of recommendations, rather than a source of problems and extra work.

All of this only works, however, if our people are truly accountable for results. If they are not accountable, they may just not tell me of problems that arise in order to get out of doing the work of solving them. Employees will not sweep problems under the rug, however, if they are accountable. Since they will be held responsible for the final product, they will do one of three things when and if they run into a problem, depending on their level of control. One is to try to solve it themselves. Another is to bring me a recommendation as to how they will solve it. And a third is to bring me an analysis of the facts, tell me they haven't the foggiest idea what to do next, and ask me for my advice. In this last case, I will give them my opinions, knowledge, ideas, and suggestions, but I will not tell them what to do. If more information is necessary, I will send them out to get it. If various alternatives need to be considered or explored, I want them to do this thinking. All of this may be followed up with a request that they bring me a recommendation as to what they will do to solve the problem.

By stressing responsibility for results in delegating, therefore, we not only pave the way for greater staff effectiveness, but we establish a climate in which reverse delegation doesn't happen.

Chapter 8

Encouraging Growth

As we have seen in previous chapters, standard management practice brings out the worst in people by frustrating two very important human needs. We have seen that when people's need for achievement is frustrated, they tend to meet that need by taking action against their employer. Such an action gives them the possibility of winning, of achieving something. Similarly, when people's need for control is frustrated, they meet that need by acting in ways that deny management's control of them. Precision Management avoids these two problems by giving employees responsibility for results and the appropriate degree of authority to decide how to achieve those results.

A third powerful need most employees bring to the workplace is the need for growth. In fact, this is in some ways the most powerful need of all.

Motivational Effects of Growth

The motivating power of growth is readily apparent when you look at new employees who haven't quite learned the job yet. While traditional managers worry about whether new employees will be able to do a good job, the employees are nonetheless enthusiastic. Once they finally have the job down pat, however, once they can do it almost without thinking, they start to lose interest in the job. Traditional managers breathe a sigh of relief when their new employees get to this stage. They say to themselves, "Whew, I'm glad I don't have to worry about his development any more." But this is precisely the time when managers ought to start worrying, because the employee's motivation is starting to lag.

One of the many places you can see this clearly is in schools. New teachers, fresh out of college, are typically given a classroom and turned loose to fend for themselves (a case of putting a person at level one on the control scale far too soon). They are both terrified and exhilarated by this experience. They are challenged but unsure of themselves because, despite their college training, they have a lot to learn. They typically stay up late, come in early, and teach quite enthusiastically. New teachers, when they get together socially, frequently complain about "the worn out old teachers" who put in minimum hours, use the same dittos they used 15 years before, and just seem to be going through the motions.

But after they have been on the job for a year or two, they get to the point where they have learned how to handle a classroom. They often begin to feel that they are in a dead-end job. There is no career ladder to climb; they don't get promoted to principal by being the best teacher. They don't receive more money than the slipshod teacher next to you by doing a better job. And gradually they, too, stop putting out their maximum effort. Their early zeal to do better, to try different approaches, to worry about doing the best job possible, begins to fade. And years later, they may greet with cynicism the enthusiasm of the new teachers who secretly complain about them.

This is of course not true of every teacher. Some do maintain their commitment and enthusiasm, gaining personal satisfaction from their ever-growing abilities. The structure of the organization does not help them do this, however, and traditionally the management methods don't either.

Another comes from the typical typing pool. As we saw in chapter two, the pool typist has one of the worst-designed jobs there is. The person has no turf, no authority for thinking, no connection with an end result. But when such people are given word-processing equipment, their enthusiasm soars. For a while. Even though the job hasn't changed, the challenge of learning to use a highly complex piece of machinery is enough to keep them interested in their work for several months. Once they become masters of the equipment and its software, however, their attitude begins to deteriorate again.

The Growth Scale

As with responsibility and control, we can define a scale on which an employee can occupy one of four positions:

1. Developing skills and attributes demanded by career.
2. Developing skills and attributes demanded by profession.
3. Developing skills and knowledge demanded by the job.
4. Not developing.

The lowest position on the scale, the one which should be a source of management concern, is the one held by the employee who isn't growing, who isn't getting anywhere or learning anything new. This is the position in which we have motivation problems, as will be discussed later.

Position three is occupied by the employee who is learning skills and information required by his job. This, as we have discussed above, is a motivating experience, and regardless of the other circumstances, the employee will look forward to the workday as long as he is learning. The problem comes when he stops learning about the job. At this stage, he will either fall back to position four or go on to one of the other two positions.

Position two is occupied by people who have learned their jobs but are developing themselves professionally. A cook, for example, might have learned how to prepare all the dishes on the menu at the restaurant he works for but may take cooking classes to develop abilities that aren't required by his present employer. Or a computer programmer whose job requires that he program an old Univac machine, might learn other programming languages that enable him to work on new microcomputers. Or a secretary might write an article about a filing system she created and go on to speak to professional organizations about this. All of these people get the satisfaction of learning something new and of feeling that they are on top of their professions. Such feelings of professionalism carry over into the doing of the job, even though the particular skills learned may not be required.

Position one on the growth scale is occupied by people who are involved in developing skills related to advancing their careers. These skills may have nothing to do with the job, as may also be the case at position two, but the skills may have nothing to do with their profession either.

A chemist, for example, who aspires to be president of his company, may go to night school to learn accounting, feeling that he will need an understanding of this field in order to fulfill his career objective. Or a hotel clerk might work nights as a waiter because knowledge of the restaurant business will help her achieve her goal of managing a hotel.

We have seen that employees are motivated by having results-oriented goals to achieve. The Winning Organization doubles this motivation by recognizing that there is another set of goals important to each employee. By openly committing themselves to helping employees achieve these personal, career goals, managers double the motivation of their people.

Symptoms of Lack of Growth

Precision Management is a powerful approach because it taps the major motivations of people and avoids the destructive behavior that results when their needs are frustrated by the job. The destructive consequences that traditional organizations struggle with when they frustrate their people's needs for growth include the decaying skills of people who have lost interest in their jobs and the out-of-date abilities of people whose professions have passed them by.

With respect to the frustration of the need for career growth, most employees fall into one of two categories. The first of these categories contains the type of employee who knows, at least in a vague sense, where he wants to go in his career but either has no sense that his current job is leading in that direction or has no explicit sense of how he will get there. The resulting frustration sometimes leads the employee to try to open an opportunity for advancement within the organization through such means as political intrigue, manipulation, discrediting of his supervisor, or similar behavior. These destructive tactics often consume much of the energy and attention of employees of traditional organizations.

The sense of frustration of this career-oriented person may become so great that eventually he is completely discouraged and gives up trying. He will say to himself "Oh, who cares." When he does so, he will find that this provides a momentary sense of relief. It feels good to throw off the impossible burden of striving. But he doesn't really not care, and eventually the frustration will creep back in. He will then tell himself he doesn't care again, and again he will find a temporary relief from his frustration.

This cycle of building frustration and relief may continue without much outward manifestation for some time, but as it progresses, the employee will find that each dose of silent "I don't care" is less effective in relieving the frustration than the last. Like a drug addict, he finds that he needs more and more frequent doses of "I don't care" to relieve his frustration. Eventually, he may find that saying it out loud provides a bigger dose of giving up. He may find other, stronger doses, such as mocking his supervisor or the organization, or coming in late. Once he starts to act out the "I don't care" attitude in these ways, he is caught in a vicious circle; his behavior insures that he will never get anywhere, producing more frustration, producing the need for bigger and bigger doses of "who cares." Alcoholism and drug abuse are sometimes turned to as the ultimate ways of throwing off the burden of frustration at not moving toward the better future the employee expected when he started his career.

Not all employees have career goals, of course. Some of those who don't may be perfectly content to stay in their present jobs, and if they are growing, either professionally or in an ever-expanding job, they may be excellent, motivated workers. Regular pay increases may help them feel they are getting somewhere in life, substituting, in a way, for moving on to higher positions of authority.

On the other hand, there are individuals who resent their position in life but have no sense that they will ever be in a better one. They tend to think of themselves as victims and of management as the victimizer. They see the future as being no doubt worse for them, not better. They tend to be found in low-skill, low-level jobs because they think of themselves as the type who will always have a lousy job, and so these are the only types of jobs they apply for. The feeling that management is out to exploit them leads them to fight back by doing the minimum and pushing the rules to the limit. "Maximum sick leave, minimum performance" seems to be the motto of such people.

This "dead-end" attitude frequently leads them to join forces with fellow victims. Such a group soothes its members by saying, in effect, that getting somewhere in life doesn't mean anything anyway, that the only thing that is important in this unfair world is to be a member of this in-group. They greet management's exhortations to work better with cynicism and non-cooperation. Their primary order of business at their "meetings" is to share new tales of victimization, so any disciplinary action taken by management only serves as grist for this mill. In fact, being disciplined or yelled at by the supervisor is guaranteed to make you the center of attention at the next meeting as the other victims gather around and say "isn't it awful how unfair they are to us." These are the people who need career goals if we are to motivate them, and they tend to be the biggest morale problems in an organization.

Standard management is interested in developing people only to the point that they are able to do a particular job. Since it is expensive and a bother to fill jobs, standard management hopes that the people who are currently able to do the jobs will stay in them forever. When managers are then confronted with the severe behavior problems that this produces for some people, they fail to understand the problem and tend to offer "demotivated" people such palliatives as more fringe benefits. They are then puzzled as to why people's attitudes don't change.

Precision Management

In the results-centered or Winning Organization, management sees that career-oriented employees will try hard to accomplish the organization's goals if they believe that those efforts will pay off in advancing their careers. As a consequence, management tries to assist employees in fulfilling career objectives, and employees put out maximum effort to succeed. The Precision Management approach, therefore, enables us to tap all three major motivators we have discussed so far: it gives employees a sense of achievement by making them accountable for results; it gives them a sense of control by giving them the authority to plan how to achieve those results; and it gives them a sense of career growth by helping employees build a track record of accomplishments which can help them advance in their careers.

Encouraging Career Growth

Precision Management thus involves helping employees clarify their career goals. The supervisor—sometimes assisted in large organizations by a professional career counselor—plays a supportive role, working with the employee to help him plan a career that will be personally satisfying. For employees who have a sense of the future being better but no concrete ideas about what type of job would be most satisfying, these sessions can unleash tremendous drive and motivation.

For those who have no sense that they will ever get anywhere, these career counseling sessions can impart a new sense of enthusiasm and hope. With this latter category, however, the supervisor should be prepared for a lengthy series of discussions. The "victim" employee is his own worst enemy, and it will usually take several discussions to get him to even consider the fact that he could get somewhere if he applied himself. After that, several more sessions will be necessary to get him to identify a satisfying career goal since he has never seriously thought about this before.

On the following page is a form which employees can use to clarify their career goals. Usually, the employee will want to do the self-analysis of the first seven steps by himself. Once the characteristics of the ideal job are generated in step eight,

CAREER GOAL-SETTING STEPS

1. Identify peak non-job experiences in your past. What are the things you have enjoyed doing the most?

2. Identify low periods in your past. What are the experiences you would wish not to re-live?

3. Thinking about your present or past jobs, imagine times when you were satisfied with your job and write some words or phrases that describe factors that led you to feel that way.

4. Imagine times when you were not satisfied with your job and write some words or phrases that identify factors that led you to feel that way.

5. Write ten words or phrases that describe yourself. For each, write what you like or dislike about being that way.

6. Prioritize the following list of characteristics of a successful life, based on what you want most from a career. If your life could be characterized by one of these qualities, which would it be: If it could be characterized by two of these, which would the second be? Prioritize the entire list based on your own feelings, not on the values others might place on them. No one will see this list but you.

   _____Belonging: to be accepted as a part of a group
   _____Duty: to fulfill life's moral obligations
   _____Expertness: to be an authority
   _____Independence: to have freedom of thought and action
   _____Leadership: to be followed and depended on by others
   _____Pleasure: to enjoy and take happiness from life's array of experiences
   _____Power: to control or exercise great influence over others
   _____Prestige: to be well known and highly regarded
   _____Security: to have a safe and stable position
   _____Actualization: to develop personal abilities to the fullest
   _____Service: to contribute to the betterment of others
   _____Wealth: to have a great deal of money

7. What are some things you've always wanted to do but never done? Include peak experiences you would like to have in life and things you would like to be able to do. Begin each with the words "I wish."

8. The answers to the first seven questions give you some criteria to use in deciding what you want from life and from a career. For example, the likes and dislikes you listed in item five are indicative of values you hold in what you want to be. Now, **without thinking of the real world or of any particular jobs,** use the values you have uncovered in the first seven steps to build the ideal job description for yourself. It is important that you do this unencumbered by your perception of what is realistic. If the world would allow you to do what you want, what kinds of things would you like to be paid to do?

9. Thinking now about real jobs, about things people get paid to do, identify one which meets as many of your criteria and comes as close to your ideal as possible.

however, the supervisor can help the employee in identifying real jobs (step nine) which have those characteristics.

Since these career goals are not secret, as they are in traditional organizations, the supervisor can spot opportunities that will help the employee gather the experience and develop the skills and personal affiliations necessary to move forward in his career. Such opportunities might include a special assignment that would help him develop those skills or membership in a club at which he could develop helpful contacts.

One of the principal advantages of the manager in The Winning Organization, therefore, is that her employees are constantly seeking additional responsibility. Delegation is thus not only easier, but more effective. Managers in traditional organizations frequently get overworked and burned out because they find "it is easier to do it myself" than to deal with the apathy and resentment that greets their assignments. In The Winning Organization, employees feel they are building a track record that will help them succeed in accomplishing their career goals, and they will seek and even demand that the manager delegate responsibility, thus freeing the manager's time for more strategic concerns.

Once the employee has determined his career goals, a "win-win" negotiation can take place between the employee and his supervisor. During this negotiation, they will determine the degree of compatibility between the employee's goals and the goals of the organization, and they will decide to what extent the organization can provide support for the attainment of those goals.

For example, imagine a secretary in city government. Imagine that after going through the nine steps of the goal-setting process, she decides that the most satisfying job for her is being an editor at a publishing house. This is a long way from her present position, and she will have to learn a lot of skills to get there. In discussing what he can do to help her succeed in her career objective, her supervisor helps her identify what responsibilities the employee might take on that would develop those skills while at the same time pursuing the goals of the organization. If the city has a newsletter which is edited by employees, for example, the secretary might be encouraged to take on that responsibility. The supervisor might also suggest that she enroll in night courses to learn editorial skills. If he knows little about editing himself, he might help her get appointments with successful editors in other organizations to talk about how to do the job or to get recommendations of useful books she might read. Whereas another employee might complain about "being stuck" with the responsibility of doing the newsletter in addition to his regular job, the secretary sees that each newsletter is a ticket to a better future. Each newsletter provides tangible evidence of her editorial abilities, and she will want to make each the best she can.

The form on the next page can be used by the employee and the supervisor to help develop a plan for the employee's career development.

As you can see, the first step in that planning process is to identify the employee's long-range career goal. This need not be the employee's ultimate job, but it should be one which is several years in the future.

The Precision Management approach to career planning is to help employees become the ideal applicant for the job they desire. Accordingly, the second step is to identify what qualities the ideal, fail-safe applicant for that job would possess. This may take some research on the employee's part, and the supervisor may be able to help point the employee to sources of information such as people who presently hire others for such positions.

In step three, the employee rates himself with respect to the ideal applicant. He identifies qualities he will need which he does not possess. Once these qualities are identified, the employee will have goals for self-development.

As indicated in the previous example of the secretary, one way to fulfill these goals for self-development is to use the present job to establish skills, knowledge, or experiences which would be helpful. The supervisor and the employee explore this possibility in step four. They may also identify affiliations (professional memberships, for example) and credentials (degrees, certifications) that the employee might pursue while working in the present job.

There may be quite a few characteristics that the employee cannot develop in the present job, however. Once these are

CAREER PLANNING STEPS

1. The job you'd eventually like to have is _____.

2. If you were hiring a person for that job, what qualities would the ideal applicant possess?

CREDENTIALS	KNOWLEDGE	SKILLS	EXPERIENCES	AFFILIATIONS

3. Rate yourself in relation to the ideal applicant. Put a check next to the credentials, knowledge, skills, experiences and affiliations you do not now possess.

4. Decide how your present job can help you get the attributes you will need to be the ideal applicant. Put a star next to those credentials, knowledge, skills, experiences, and affiliations you can develop while holding your present job.

5. List interim jobs that could help you get the credentials, knowledge, skills, experiences, or affiliations you need.

6. For which of those jobs could your present job most adequately prepare you?

7. If you were hiring a person for that job, what qualities would the ideal applicant possess?

CREDENTIALS	KNOWLEDGE	SKILLS	EXPERIENCES	AFFILIATIONS

8. Which of these attributes do you not now possess? Place a check next to them.

9. Which of the checked qualities will not be developed through your present job?

10. List educational or volunteer opportunities you could seize in order to develop the needed attributes.

identified, the next step is to identify jobs that could help the employee develop those qualities. These become interim steps on the employee's career path.

In step six, the supervisor helps the employee identify which of these interim jobs the present job can most adequately prepare him for. This becomes the employee's immediate career objective. They then analyze that job in terms of the qualities the ideal applicant would possess and rate the employee in relation to those attributes. The present job is then analyzed in terms of how well it can prepare the employee to be the ideal applicant. The supervisor may identify special task-forces or additional responsibilities not normally part of the job that the employee could undertake in order to prepare himself.

Lastly, if there are still some qualities that the employee needs which cannot be developed within the context of his job, the supervisor will help him identify educational or volunteer opportunities that could help. Using the instance of the secretary who wants to be an editor, for example, if the organization has no newsletter of its own, the supervisor might help the employee find a non-profit agency who needs a volunteer to edit its newsletter. He might also help her identify college courses she could take in order to develop credentials that would help her fulfill her role in the future. And he might refer her to other employees in the organization who have mastered certain competencies and to whom she can turn for advice and assistance.

Traditional managers tend to resist this kind of role, in part because they fear losing a good employee whose next logical career step takes him outside the organization. As discussed previously, they tend to try to keep employees in one place as long as possible.

Results-oriented managers, on the other hand, recognize that they will get better work from the employee who sees that what he is doing helps not only the organization but his own career. They also encounter more employee willingness to accept additional responsibilities; the common refusal of non-growing employees to take on such responsibility ("That's not in my job description.") is not heard from the worker who sees that the job is getting him somewhere. The benefit to both the individual and the organization from this synergy is a more concerted and committed effort toward the attainment of individual and organizational goals.

One of the advantages of this approach is that it responds to the job mobility of today's professionals. Increasingly, white collar workers have come to look at a career as encompassing experiences with several employers. Effective managers take full advantage of the talents of such workers while they, in turn, take full advantage of the work experiences that will help advance their careers. While accommodating the employee who may stay with the organization for one to ten years, this approach also responds fully to the worker whose career objectives can be met fully within the organization and who stays on until retirement.

One question which is often raised by traditional managers about such a system is "What if everyone wants to be president of the company? Won't many of them get discouraged?" Such a question confuses career goals with climbing a particular organization's hierarchy (as in traditional organizations' "career ladder" models). An employee's career goal to be president of a large (or small) company can be satisfied in many organizations, not just by the one he is presently working for.

If the organization has twelve such "people on the move," for example, it is very fortunate, for their personal drive to succeed will reap great rewards for the organization. As opportunities for promotion arise, only one of the twelve will be promoted at a time, presumably the best of the lot. Others, who in traditional organizations might begin to wage political guerrilla war to advance themselves or who might otherwise become "demotivated" by the experience, will be encouraged by the results-oriented manager not to get frustrated by looking only at the one job they didn't get; rather they will be encouraged to look at the thousands of such jobs that exist in the community (or nation) as a whole and to continue to prepare for such a job by establishing a track record of outstanding performance. As a consequence, their morale stays high, and they continue to produce results. The standard approach of discouraging or ignoring career growth may keep these people around for a few more years, but they will be people stagnating, and as a consequence, they will not produce the achievements possible through Precision Management methods.

In fact, the results-oriented manager is very wary of having people around who are not growing. She is careful, when hiring, to avoid hiring victims, to hire only "people on the move." Such people ensure that the organization will be an "organization on the move" and that the manager herself will be establishing the kind of track record that guarantees her own career progress. This management style creates an alliance between the supervisor and employee for their mutual benefit and ensures that the organization gets maximum results. In traditional organizations, by contrast, the supervisor is often seen as the enemy, and results, in light of employee resistance, are obtained only with great management effort.

Encouraging Professional Growth

Similarly, employees will perform better if the organization encourages their professional growth. Means of doing this include paying employees' memberships in professional organizations, encouraging employees to try out new approaches to doing their jobs, encouraging them to write articles for publication in professional journals, paying employees' fees to conventions and conferences, encouraging attendance at relevant seminars, and paying for additional higher education. Most of these methods are also employed by traditional organizations.

Other means of encouraging professional growth include encouraging visits to other organizations within the community, asking the employee to prepare a research paper on a given subject, and asking an employee to prepare and present a training session for other employees on a matter related to the profession. This last is a particularly effective method because it demands that the employee become an expert in the particular skill being taught. The organization benefits from all of this because the employee becomes a more skilled individual and also because the sense of professional growth, of being on top of his profession, produces pride and motivation to do his job with excellence.

Encouraging Growth from Job Experiences

The effective supervisor can also encourage employees' growth during the monitoring interviews. In chapter three, we discussed how these interviews are set up at certain checkpoints. At these checkpoints the employee reports his progress to his supervisor. As indicated previously, that progress will be either "on-target" or "off-target." The effective supervisor uses either situation to encourage employee learning.

We often hear it said that "people learn from experience," but in fact, they don't always. Many keep making the same mistakes over again or fail to profit from their successes. Further, in traditional organizations, one employee will often make a mistake which was made earlier by another employee. Using standard management techniques, the supervisor must take pains to ferret out the reasons for the mistakes (which employees often try to hide from their superior) and then communicate them to the rest of the group. Supervisors using Precision Management methods help employees learn from their mistakes and their successes, both individually and as a group.

Learning from experience involves three steps. First, we "identify" the experience; we do not learn from an experience unless we can describe it to ourselves or to others. Second, we "analyze" the experience; we think about why the experience occurred and why it had the characteristics it had. And finally we draw some generalizations that apply beyond the single experience.

To help an employee grow in the job, the supervisor should keep these three steps—identify, analyze, and generalize—in mind. At the checkpoints, and at other times as well, she can review the employee's experiences in this three step format. Such a review should not be rigidly bound to the format; it may go back and forth among the three steps, but by keeping the format in mind, the manager can readily facilitate an employee's growth while simultaneously monitoring progress and helping the organization get better results.

For example, let's imagine that I supervise a woman whose responsibility at my consulting firm is getting new contracts for the

company.   One of the activities she engages in to do that is to
write proposals for new business to local government organizations.   She submits a plan for the year as to how much business
she will generate for the firm, and I approve it.   Since she has been
with me for a while, and I am generally impressed with the way
she carries out her responsibilities (meaning she always does the
kind of thing I want done), I don't want to waste my time
approving her marvelous recommendations, so I put her at level
two on the control scale (the authority for self-assignment
provided the boss is kept informed).   At her first checkpoint for
the year, however, I find that she is off-target.

The first task (as far as her growth is concerned) is to get her to
identify her experience in attempting to achieve her result.   I ask
her, therefore, to tell me in some detail what she did during the
period.   She explains that she spent most of the time working on a
proposal to a unit of state government to conduct $12,000 worth
of management training.   She felt confident she would be
successful since we had done other training for this agency, and
they were quite enthusiastic about it.   Unfortunately, however, the
agency decided to contract with another firm.

When I ask her why she thinks this happened (the analyzing
step), she (being a smart person) already has discovered the
reason.   If she hadn't yet figured this out, I might have to do a lot
of probing, and we might have to interrupt the interview for a day
or two while she gathered the facts.   But she already has gathered
the facts.   She explains, with frustration, that although our cost
was lower than that of the successful bidder, the winners had
proposed using a number of films in their seminar.   She thinks this
is a stupid reason for selecting them over us, but this is
nonetheless the case.

Now I ask, "If you had to do this over again, knowing what you
know now, what would you do differently?" (More analyzing).   She
thinks a moment and then says, "I guess I probably would have
figured out how to put some films into our training program." I
like this answer, because it is just the kind of thing I would have
said, so we go on to looking for a generalization.

"Is there anything you will do differently in the future, now that you've had this experience?"

She thinks a moment. "I guess I could look at the kinds of proposals a client has funded before to see if they seem to have any biases. Except they funded us before, and we didn't have a film in that workshop."

Back to analyzing: "Is there any difference between the workshop they funded and the one they didn't?"

"Well, the one they didn't was a longer workshop. Maybe that was the difference."

Back to searching for a generalization: "Is there any other thing you could do to make sure this doesn't happen to us again?"

"I guess I could talk to them beforehand to try to feel them out about what they'd like to see in the proposal."

"Okay. That sounds like a good rule to me. Remember, your job isn't just to write proposals. I can get winos in here for a fraction of the cost to write proposals. Your job is to get additional business for the company, and you have the job because you are so capable. It sounds like this new rule of yours will help you do even better than you've done in the past."

We then examine whether we need to change her proposed target, the proposed amount of business she feels she can generate, given this setback. She feels she can still reach the target, so we leave it to review again at the next checkpoint.

At that next meeting, she is pleased and excited to report that she is back on-target and in fact may well exceed her target if things continue to go so well. I, of course, congratulate her, but my role includes more than merely giving her recognition (though that is important). My role is to make sure she continues to grow, to get better. So I want to make sure that she learns from her successes as well as her failures.

So after she recounts her experiences I ask (to encourage analysis) "Why do you think you were so successful this time?" She responds that she applied the rule of sounding out the client before she wrote the proposal and that it seems to be working.

"Is there anything else that you've done differently?" I ask. This is back to identifying. I do this because I want to make sure that we don't lose something valuable.

She thinks for a minute. "Well, I've started including an executive summary of the main points of the proposal at the beginning."

"How would that have helped?" (Back to analyzing.)

"Well I did it on a long proposal so that people would know the big picture before they started reading the details. I thought it might help them understand it better as they read along."

"How else might it have helped in the long proposal?" (More analyzing)

"I don't know."

"If you were reading a bunch of proposals, which would be more appealing, one with a summary or one without?" (Still analyzing.)

She thinks again. "Gee, I never looked at it from their angle before. I guess it might be pretty difficult to grasp some of the concepts. And pretty overwhelming to have to read several long proposals. Maybe ours was the only one they could understand."

"At least it took less effort to understand it."

"Right."

Now for the generalizing part. "Is there any rule you can think of here that you should follow in the future."

"Always add a summary?"

"Something broader than that. A general principle that this is just one example of."

She thinks. "Make it easy on the proposal reader?"

We have now succeeded in helping her learn more completely from her success. We have helped her identify parts of the experience that might have otherwise been lost and to pull a particular lesson from them that might not have been learned. I want her to begin to apply this principle, so I close the meeting with "Sounds good to me. Think about other ways you could do that and try them out before our next meeting."

Concentrating on growth not only helps keep your employees motivated, but it helps make the job of the manager much less frustrating. If you concentrate directly on the output of your people, if that is where you get your satisfaction, then you will be frustrated as a manager whenever your people are less able to do the work than you are. Standard management practice is born of this frustration, because when managers see that employees are less able to achieve results than they are themselves, they tend to handle their frustration in one of two disastrous ways: they either try to do the important jobs themselves, which overloads them and discourages the worker, or they take away their people's control, which leads to resentment and apathy.

Odd as it may sound on the surface, a results-oriented manager who uses Precision Management methods doesn't focus directly on the results her people achieve. She doesn't get her satisfaction from their success directly but leaves that to them to savor. Rather she gets her satisfaction, and avoids frustration, by concentrating on the growth of her people. If, as managers, we concentrate on this, if we concentrate not on absolute success or failure but on our people growing from the attempt, then management becomes less frustrating and more effective. It becomes less frustrating because we can get satisfaction from their improvement even if they are not perfect. And we become more effective because if our people are growing, if they are getting better and better, then the results we get through them will continue to get better and better, and we will find our job as manager easier and easier to do. An effective manager's primary product, then, is the growth of her people.

Growth Meetings

We can also employ this approach in helping the entire unit learn from the mistakes and success of its members. To do this, the results-oriented manager holds periodic staff meetings to encourage growth and communication and to plan for the future. The frequency of such staff meetings depends on many factors, such as how important it is for employees to work together and how comfortable the manager is with their performance. As we will see, the meeting not only encourages the collective learning of the group but uses that learning as a key factor in the goal-setting process. In any case, no less often than once per quarter and no more often than once every two weeks, the manager holds a meeting with the following eleven-step agenda:

1. Review Purpose of Organization
2. Review Purpose of Unit
3. Review Goals of Unit

These first three steps can be covered in a few sentences and should consume almost no time at the meeting. The reason for doing this is to focus everyone on outcomes, on the real reason they are there so as to avoid getting bogged down in activity-centered concerns.

4. Review Experiences of the Preceding Period

Here, all employees will recount their attempts to accomplish their objectives during the preceding period. Those who have succeeded will get recognition from their peers; those who failed will get sympathy. If the manager supervises a very large staff, she may have only some of the employees report at this stage and others at a later meeting.

5. Identify What Has Been Learned

All employees will come to the meeting knowing that they are not being held accountable for 100 percent perfect performance but for learning from their attempts to achieve perfect performance. For this reason, the manager doesn't have to worry that she will find lies, distortions, and withheld facts at step four. In any case, all will know that the focus of the meeting is on growth. Each employee will therefore come to the meeting prepared to share what he or she has learned from the success or the failure reported in step four. The manager may facilitate this process by using the experience-identify-analyze-generalize model described previously. As each reports, other employees can learn from his experiences, and all can grow together, avoiding the mistakes of their peers and profiting from the lessons of their co-workers' success. The remaining steps of the process use this learning as a basis for future action.

6. Re-examine and Modify (if necessary) Goals

At this stage, the manager asks, "Based on what we have learned, do we have to modify, add to, or delete any of our goals?"

Precision Management

She conducts a discussion of this with her people, though the final decision on this matter still rests with her.

7. Identify Problems and Opportunities in the
    Up-coming Period

Again, the manager's role is to have the right questions, not all the answers. Her people are the ones doing the job, and they know the day-to-day situation better than she. So she asks the group "What problems do you see coming up in the period ahead?" And "What opportunities do you see?" If necessary to spur discussion, she asks each employee these questions directly.

8. Propose Accomplishments for the Next Period

She then asks the question which brings all of this together and focuses the meeting on action: "Based on what we have learned, on our goals, on the problems and opportunities we have identified, what should we be trying to accomplish in the next period?" She can add items herself during the ensuing discussion, but it is best if the ideas come from staff members. They will pursue ideas more energetically and feel better about their work if they feel a sense of ownership of these objectives. Employees should be encouraged to think creatively at this point, to brainstorm as many ideas as possible. None will be discussed critically at this stage, and anything anyone says will be considered a valid contribution.

9. Prioritize Proposed Accomplishments

At this step, the manager asks, "Which of these should we consider top priority?" As each item is identified, some discussion of its importance may take place. The manager still has veto power, of course, and can unilaterally state that something will be of top priority, but again, she involves her people in the process; she knows that if it comes from them, they will do a better job.

10. Facilitate and Direct Self-Assignment of Top
     Priority Tasks

At this step, the manager again relies on having the right questions. She goes through the list of top priority tasks and asks "Who's going to do this?" People then are involved in choosing their assignments. She can assign a person to a task ("Mary, I'd like you to handle this one"), but, as before, she is better off if they do most of this themselves.

11. Make Individual Appointments with Each Employee

The manager closes the meeting by making individual appointments with each employee. At these individual meetings, she will define the degree of control they are authorized to exercise in pursuit of their responsibilities and will define how their success is to be measured. If the employee is at level three on the control scale in pursuing this assignment, the manager will ask the employee when they can meet to review the employee's plan of action. And she will also establish checkpoints at which each worker's progress is reviewed. This individual meeting also provides an opportunity to discuss the assignment: the employee can ask questions and the manager can share information she has about the task.

By following these eleven steps, the manager keeps things under control and encourages the growth of all staff members in the pursuit of the organization's goals. The process keeps the organization viable in the face of changing conditions.

The process also facilitates the formation of task forces around major issues affecting the organization. At one hospital, for example, managers were concerned about the extremely competitive environment in which they operated. One of the problems identified by employees in going through a version of this process was a lack of sensitivity to patients on the part of some employees. A task force was formed with the goal of increasing patient satisfaction with the the way they were treated at the hospital. Membership on the task force was voluntary and members were drawn from a variety of departments. As they pursued their goal—developing new systems of making patients feel welcome, identifying the causes of insensitive behavior, conducting problem-solving sessions—members not only helped overcome one of the hospital's major obstacles to success but experienced the motivation that comes from learning much new information and mastered new skills.

Growth and Job Design

Another approach to encouraging growth on the job is to design the job so that the employee can grow in it for quite some time. In chapter two, we saw how a supermarket manager can increase job satisfaction and profits by giving each clerk expanded responsibilities for planning and evaluating the work. Jobs designed in this way also provide the individual clerks with long-term possibilities for growth.

As stated before, their new responsibilities need not be given them all at once: the clerks would not have sufficient skill or knowledge of the grocery business to take on all the new tasks at first. The first responsibility they could be given might be to keep an eye on the supply of merchandise on their shelves and to restock it whenever they saw it was necessary. When the clerks proved to the store manager that they had mastered that task, they could be given the next logical responsibility, that of keeping track of inventories in the store room and for ordering new stock when they ran low. This was again something new to learn. When the motivating power of that wore off, when they had mastered that, they could be given the new challenge of the responsibility for displaying the merchandise, then for allotting shelf space, then for determining customer buying preferences, and so on.

As the clerks mastered these tasks, and the profits of their individual aisles improved, the store manager could afford to increase their salaries, preferably in accordance with the increase in their profits. This would help clerks get the feeling they were "getting somewhere" personally, thus avoiding the dead-end syndrome.

As the clerks developed their new skills, the store manager would find he had developed a number of competent grocery professionals. He would find therefore, that he had developed a base on which to expand his business by opening a new store. The clerk who had the best record of sales might be given the job of managing the new store. Gradually, he could open other stores, with his experienced grocery professionals moving up in their careers. Eventually, he would find that his investment in developing the talents of his people not only made his job easier and his original store more profitable, but it would allow him to build a chain of successful stores.

Such an application of Precision Management principles leads employees to get the satisfaction of career growth as well as the satisfaction of job growth. As has been discussed in earlier chapters, it also gives them the satisfaction of achievement and of control.

This example shows how the Precision Management approach works as a whole and in action. Of necessity, the individual features of the system have been presented piecemeal, but each part of the system works in concert with the rest. In order for the clerks to grow, they first have to have a job in which their turf was defined (their aisle). The approach also requires that they have results to achieve (one being to increase profits) and that they have access to the information necessary to control their work. The manager then turns over, bit by bit, the thinking tasks that had been his exclusive province in the past, gradually empowering his employees and increasing the employee's control. As they succeed in carrying out each new responsibility, the manager gives them lots of encouragement (described further in the next chapter) and gives them a bit more control.

Everybody wins from this approach. By managing this way, the store owner makes his job easier to do, increases the profitability of his venture, gives better service to his customers, and allows all of his clerks to get maximum satisfaction from what is often a very dull, dead-end job.

Chapter 9

Motivation and Recognition

When workers want to do the job, management is much easier and the organization gets better results. Workers want to do the job when doing the job satisfies a need of theirs. For most modern workers, there are four major needs.

We have already discussed three of these motivational needs— the needs for achievement, for control, and for growth—and we have seen how Precision Management succeeds in tapping them. Each is powerful, and the positive effects are long-lasting. The need for achievement, for example, lasts as long as the worker is striving to attain a result. Each can be employed with relatively little management effort. In this chapter, we will examine the fourth major motivator, the need for recognition, a motivator which is very different in character from the other three.

Of all the needs workers have, the need for recognition is the most gluttonous. It needs to be fed constantly. In studies of motivation, recognition has been shown to have the greatest impact but the shortest duration. While a pat on the back may make a worker feel terrific today, tomorrow the effect will start to wear off, and the next day it will be lost entirely.

In traditional organizations, there is often a disparity of opinion between the workers and management as to whether the workers are valued and appreciated, the workers frequently feeling that management doesn't know the quality of the workers' performance or doesn't value their skill and efforts. Part of this difference of perception comes from management's misunderstanding about the duration of recognition. A manager who tells workers one month that he is proud of their work will expect that workers will continue to feel appreciated the next month. For the worker, however, the feeling of appreciation wears off a few days after the remark is made. The manager is under the illusion that the workers know he values their work and is thus baffled when he hears they feel unappreciated.

Unproductive Ways of Getting Recognition

As with the other needs we've talked about, workers will either get the need for recognition met productively, through the job, or unproductively. One unproductive way (from the organization's point of view) that workers may meet their needs for recognition is to make off-the-job concerns, such as games or playing the stock market, their highest personal priority. An employee may devote himself to bowling, for example, in which case much of his time spent at work is actually spent thinking about improving his score and winning his bowling partners' recognition.

In other cases, employees may meet their needs for recognition in ways that are destructive to the organization. In making fun of their supervisor, for example, employees may get laughter (and hence recognition) from their peers. This need, as indicated above, must be fed constantly, so such employees tend to engage in acts great and small on a regular basis that thwart the organization.

Such recognition for destructive acts can therefore be an added reward for the destructive ways of meeting the other three needs. In doing something negative to assert his control, for example, an employee may draw the cheers of his comrades who have similar feelings of frustration, thereby satisfying his need for recognition. Employees with powerful needs for advancement, who see they are getting nowhere, may give up in such dramatic ways (such as saying "who cares?" when the boss is talking) that they draw the laughter of their comrades or the admiration of the in-group of dead-enders. This recognition reinforces the "acting-out" behavior. Employees who submit grievances in order to meet their needs for achievement may also be patted on the back by their peers when they win. These "unmotivated" people, as we have said before, are in fact highly motivated. They are motivated by the same needs that drive "motivated" people; the difference is that they have found it easier to meet these needs in counter-productive ways because of the way the work is planned, organized, and managed.

One of the reasons the traditional boss doesn't give workers recognition as often as he should is that he is unsure how much a comment from him would mean to his people. He is unsure of their respect for him or unsure of himself. In the midst of this insecurity, he overlooks how important recognition is to most people. Even if workers don't respect the boss, being told that they have done a good job means a lot. They will talk about it that night at home. And still feel good about it the next day. The following day, however, they will need another boost.

For this reason, the boss needs a variety of means of recognition at her disposal. Saying "good job, Joe," will make Joe feel good today, but after he's heard it 20 times or more, he will get a little tired of it or even a little suspicious about the sincerity with which the comment was made. Managers in an effective organization thus have a variety of means of recognizing employees at their disposal, from small, daily methods, to more substantial rewards, to big, yearly prizes.

Levels of Recognition

We are all familiar with the big, splashy types of recognition. One sales organization gives luxury automobiles to its top performers. An international manufacturer gives its best factory workers a trip to visit company plants in foreign countries. One city public works department arranged with a local Ford dealer to contribute the use of a new Thunderbird for two weeks to the outstanding worker of the year. (The dealer got the advantage of free advertising because the award was mentioned in the media.)

A major problem with such awards, at least in traditional organizations, is that they are not always based on objective standards of performance. Workers themselves know who the best workers are, and if an employee who is not the best worker gets an "employee of the year" award, the effect of such an award can be demoralizing to the rest of the work force. In recognition of this, some traditional organizations have had workers themselves select the recipient of the award. Such a system avoids the charges of management favoritism but can also run into problems. If the work force as a whole is hostile, for example, the workers might deliberately chose the employee who is the biggest thorn in the side of management as the recipient of the award. Or they may fall prey to their own favoritism, never giving the award to a top performer who is not part of the in-group. In response to these difficulties, one group of workers I know routinely gives the "employee of the year" award to the employee who is closest to retirement.

In The Winning Organization, workers are measured on the basis of objective criteria. As described in earlier chapters, these criteria are related to the output of their efforts. As a result, everyone always knows who the most successful worker is, and giving awards on the basis of excellence is easy to do.

Such major rewards, however, are only a small part of an effective program of employee recognition. For one thing, they come too infrequently to provide the continual slaking of the thirst for recognition that most workers require. And of necessity, they apply to only a small portion of the work force in that they are reserved for the truly outstanding workers.

In response to the need for more frequent recognition, many organizations have instituted a series of minor rewards for good performance. "Employee of the month" certificates, sending top performers to conventions or seminars, victory parties in honor of a major achievement, and birthday celebrations ("We're glad you're in the world and are with us.") are examples of such recognition. One organization has meetings every quarter in which each person comes armed with a positive thing to say about every other staff person. The meeting consists of the sharing of these statements.

But even this isn't enough. The challenge to management is to come up with innovative, daily recognition of employee contributions. These things are usually so small that the traditional manager overlooks them. But their importance cannot be understated. Years ago, when I worked for a consulting firm in Washington, D.C., I noticed that my office mate was very upset one day. All day long, she was unable to concentrate on her work with her usual level of commitment. After some prodding, she finally told me what was bothering her. She said that the boss always smiled and said "good morning" to her when she arrived but that that day he had just stared at her as though she wasn't even there.

Our boss was totally oblivious to this. No doubt, the change in his behavior was because he was preoccupied with the problems of the day. And had this been called to his attention, he would have been amazed at the large response to such a minor incident. Again, we as managers are too humble; we don't realize how much a word or a gesture from us means to the morale of our people.

By developing a comprehensive program of employee recognition which combines all three types of recognition, The Winning Organization develops pride, commitment, and loyalty in its people.

Some Ideas for Recognizing Employees

A few examples of daily, intermediate, and yearly rewards are listed on the following page. The list is, of course, far from exhaustive. It is presented in order to spur your ideas about different ways of recognizing employees in your situation. As you think of new ideas, record them on a master list so you have as large a repertory of methods as possible.

One way to remind yourself to do this as often as it is necessary is to make a chart, such as the one below, which enables you to keep track of when and how you have recognized your employees. Looking at this each day will help you to feed, in a variety of ways, your people's voracious need for recognition. The blank spaces on the chart are used to make a brief note of what you did to recognize each employee.

DATE	JOHN	MARY	SUSAN	FRANK	EFREN

IDEAS FOR RECOGNIZING EMPLOYEES

DAILY MEANS OF RECOGNIZING EMPLOYEES

Saying "Thank You."
Telling them they did a good job.
Suggesting they join you for coffee.
Asking for their opinions.
Greeting them when they come in in the morning.
Showing interest in their ideas.
Smiling when you see them.
Bragging about them to your boss (in their presence).
Jotting small thank you notes to them.
Saying "Good night."
Having a refreshment with them after work.
Talking to them about how their day went.
Saying something positive about their personal qualities.
Showing interest in their personal lives.

INTERMEDIATE MEANS OF RECOGNIZING EMPLOYEES

Taking them to lunch.
Letting them put their names on the products they produce.
Buying the first pitcher of beer for "the best crew of the month."
Writing them a letter of commendation (with copies to personnel file
    and other appropriate people).
Getting a radio station they listen to to mention them.
Putting them on important task-forces.
Giving the best parking space to the "employee of the month."
Posting graphic displays, showing progress toward targets.
Mentioning major contributors by name in your status reports to your
    boss or to those higher up.
Have them present their results to higher-ups.
Giving permission to go to a seminar, convention, or professional
    meeting, if possible at the organization's expense.
Writing newsletter articles about their performance.
Having them present a training session to co-workers.
Celebrating their birthdays.
Having your boss write them a letter of thanks.
Celebrating major accomplishments.
Having them represent you at important meetings.
Sending letters of thanks to their families.

MAJOR MEANS OF RECOGNIZING EMPLOYEES

Make special caps, shirts, belt buckeles, or pins honoring them.
Encouraging them to write an article about some accomplishment at work.
Giving them a plaque, certificate, or trophy for being best employee,
    best crew, most improved, etc.
Giving them a raise.
Giving them a bigger office.
Getting their picture in the paper for an outstanding accomplishment.
Giving additional responsibilities and a new title.
Giving them new equipment.
Rent billboard or newspaper space to thank them.

Recognition and Levels of Control

The preceding chart is particularly useful when you are dealing with people who are operating at level one on the control scale. Level three people have natural recognition built in to the management relationship; every time they make an acceptable recommendation, they get recognition for it in the form of your approval. Level two people also have natural opportunities for recognition when they make their progress reports (as do level three and even level four people when they make their progress reports). When we have people working at level one, however, we need to take special care to make sure that they are getting the recognition they need.

Major means of recognition still work for people at level one. The major rewards mentioned above can be given for accomplishing the results they are working toward. (We don't require plans or progress reports of people at level one, but we do know what they are trying to achieve, and we do learn of their final accomplishments.) It is the daily, verbal recognition that we need to take special pains to make sure they get.

Because we don't know the daily successes of the person, there is no natural opportunity to say things like "good job." We can, however, do and say things about the qualities of the person. Smiles, pats on the back, and daily greetings serve to let the employee know he is appreciated regardless of whether the employee has done something outstanding. Similarly, statements which affirm that we think the person is smart, capable, responsible, creative, and so forth have a positive motivational effect which can substitute for recognition for a particular action. As we will see in the next chapter, such phrases also contribute to the employee's self-image and lead him to maintain the top performance he has demonstrated. When you tell someone he is responsible, for example, it makes him feel good and tends to lead to his looking around for responsible things to do to prove you are right.

Individual Differences

In addition to considering the level of control the employee exercises, effective managers also consider the type of recognition that will appeal to a given person. Traditional managers tend to rely on the same types of rewards for all employees—flowers for all secretaries, plaques for all salesmen, and so forth. But just as a person who is a fanatic about one game may not care for another at all, people are different in the value they place on various types of recognition. One person I know, for example, will do practically anything if he knows he will get a certificate for doing a good job. You can get a clue to this by looking at the hundreds of certificates he has framed on his office wall. Another person I know, however, throws certificates away. To him, they are just more paper to clutter up his office.

There are even a few people who do not want any recognition at all. Such people regard recognition as something that is needed by insecure people. They have developed their own internal sense of personal strength to the point where they are the source of their own rewards. Managers who tell such a person "Gee, that's excellent work; that is really good; keep it up," are regarded as irritating rather than as rewarding. These people know they did a good job and don't require anyone else to tell them so.

Such self-sufficiency is rare in the workplace, but does occur occasionally. It is a phenomenon to look for if your recognition of a particular employee seems to be having a negative effect. In our discussion of all the major motivators, we have been talking about needs that the vast majority of today's workers have. Part of the art of management is to diagnose which needs are most important for which people. For some people, some of these may have little impact.

The effective manager, therefore, gets to know employees' individual preferences and values in this area. She does this by taking a personal interest in each employee she supervises, in itself a form of recognition. This also helps her make judgments on which employees can handle what assignments and to treat each in the way that is most likely to spur him to top performance.

Precision Management

Precision Management is about getting results from people. It is easiest to do this if you know them well.

A Proviso

Recognition is only effective if it is given out of genuine respect for the worker and the value of his efforts. Praising a worker for a job which is not well-done is self-defeating. The worker himself knows the quality of the work and will either come to the conclusion that you have low standards or will assume that you are trying to manipulate him. It also dilutes the sincere praise you give to others. None of this makes a positive contribution to achieving good results from your people.

One supervisor told me that he had a hopeless worker who did not respond to any of his motivational efforts. In desperation, he tried giving the worker an outstanding rating in his performance review to see if that would work. When that did not work, he fired the person. The worker then sued the organization for unfairly firing him. The court found in the worker's favor because the supervisor had praised his work so highly on his performance review.

The effective manager looks for that in the workers performance which can be praised. Instead of trying to catch the worker doing something unacceptable, the effective manager tries to catch her workers doing something praiseworthy. "Find the good and praise it" is the motto of such a person. But if the worker's performance cannot be praised in any meaningful way, it is a mistake to give him recognition. Such cases should be subject to corrective action, a topic we will address in chapter eleven.

Chapter 10

Strengthening Employee Self-image

People tend to be consistent. John tends to behave "like John;" Mary just "like Mary." When our people behave in outstanding ways, this consistency is a blessing, but when they perform poorly, it becomes a problem for us as supervisors. Faced with consistently unacceptable performance, we find ourselves with the difficult problem of getting them to change their behavior, to behave in ways that aren't usually "like them."

By following the organizational principles in the first part of this book, we create conditions which help employees want to do their best. If we do a good job of establishing a structure in which employees have clear responsibility for results, have some sense of ownership of those results, have the appropriate degree of control over the means of achieving those results, and are measured by their degree of success, then we will have far fewer performance problems than our competitors. All these are external conditions which affect performance and which are relatively easy for us to control.

There is another set of conditions, however, that affects an employee's disposition to do the work. These are conditions within the employee that prevent him from fulfilling his true potential. These are the beliefs about the self, beliefs about what is "like me" that he brings to the job. The employee's beliefs about who he is have a hidden but extremely important effect on how well he performs because they control what he perceives about the world, how he behaves, and how much of his true potential he can achieve.

In order to get results through others, a manager must be concerned with all factors that affect her ability to do so. The average manager, however, doesn't see that the employee's beliefs about himself have anything to do with the job of managing. She is not very aware of the problem such beliefs create for her in getting the job done, and she is totally unaware that she affects those beliefs in unthinking ways every day. Not thinking about her effect on her employees' beliefs, she will tend to follow her natural instincts in dealing with their behavior. And typically, as we will see, this means she will affect those beliefs in ways that make matters worse.

Selective Perception

One of the ways in which an employee's self-beliefs affect his performance is in the way he views the environment in which he performs. Beliefs about the self affect our perception of reality because of the way the conscious mind works. At any given moment, the conscious mind is capable of attending to only a small portion of the total stimuli received by the body's sensory apparatus. Our brains are constantly being bombarded by a lot of stimuli that we are consciously unaware of—the speed of the heart, the smell of the air, the feel of the chair, information from every hair follicle on the body, and so on. While the subconscious mind can handle and process all of this information, the conscious mind's capacity is much more limited. It needs to have this information filtered and simplified. This is generally a good thing, because it lets us concentrate on important things, and it keeps us from the insanity that trying to cope with too much information would bring.

While we are concentrating on a few things, however, we fill in the background with assumptions about the rest of the environment. These assumptions come from our beliefs about the environment. To the extent that these beliefs do not match the reality of the situation, we perceive the world in a distorted fashion.

The possibilities of distortion are increased by the filtering process itself. When the subconscious mind filters out the majority of the stimuli, it does so based on what it believes to be "of value." We are generally unaware of our heart beat, for example, but if it skips a beat, our heart rate suddenly becomes information "of value," and our conscious mind attends to it. The problem is that things that do not fit our view of the world are not considered "of value" and tend to get filtered out.

We all tend to see the world, therefore, as we expect it to be. Our expectations about it tend to be self-fulfilling. And our expectations stem from our beliefs about ourselves and the world in relation to ourselves.

Because employees see what they expect to see, their self-beliefs and self-images affect the organization's success. If an employee believes, for example, that he is the kind of person who never has "the luck" to discover any major opportunities, he will tend not to see opportunities when they appear in the environment. He will either filter the opportunities out entirely, or he will distort them and treat them as problems to be gotten rid of. His own belief blinds him as surely as physical disability.

Similarly, an employee who believes that life is unfair and fraught with problems will tend to affect the organization negatively because of the way he perceives the world. Expecting to find problems, he will tend to concentrate on why things can't work instead of on finding new ideas for improvement. He will see myriad difficulties in the way things are, but he will offer no hope that things can be better. He will be unable to spot opportunities for growth for himself or for his organization because to do so wouldn't be like him and "like him" is the only way he behaves. Such an employee, despite his abilities to do the job itself, is a brake on the wheel of progress. His hidden beliefs about himself not only limit his own possibilities but keeps the organization from achieving its full potential.

Beliefs and Behavior

Beliefs not only control how we perceive reality, but they also limit and control our behavior. An employee who believes that he always makes a fool of himself in front of strangers will continue to behave in embarrassed and embarrassing ways whenever the organization needs him to interact with outside persons. No matter what his technical skills and knowledge, no matter how well he may grasp the content of his presentation, the picture he has of himself will prevent him from behaving in an outstanding manner. The picture he sees in his mind is not one of his success but of his failure. He fears and dwells on the possibility of behaving awkwardly. It is "like him" to behave that way, and as he prepares for the important meeting, he pictures doing poorly.

This mental rehearsal for failure prepares him well to fail. When he walks into the meeting, he expects to do poorly. He may hope to do better than usual, but his hopes and wishes are up against a formidable obstacle, an obstacle that exists not in the external world but in the internal beliefs the person holds about what is like him.

He then tends to view reality through the filter of these beliefs. As he enters the room full of strangers, for example, he may interpret their facial expressions as indicating disdain for him. If, by chance, someone is smiling, he will tend to filter that out. It doesn't fit his expectation and so is discarded by the subconscious mind, which is in charge of maintaining a consistent self-image and world-view. Moreover, he makes assumptions about the many factors on which his conscious mind is incapable of concentrating. He assumes that all of these factors are in accordance with his expectations about the situation, and these expectations stem from his belief that he will not do well.

As he makes his presentation, he will try to succeed, but he will tend to behave in accordance with his picture of what is like him. Just as a hypnotized person is unable to move when he is told his shoes are nailed to the floor, his beliefs about the situation constrain his actions. Even if he does better than usual, his selective perception of the event will tend to reinforce the belief that, once again, he has not done well. After the meeting, he dwells on the negative aspects of the experience. Anything positive is ignored as he stews in a cauldron of negative images.

Strengthening of Present Beliefs

The belief is then further fortified by the self-talk that goes on in his head. "Boy, these people think I'm a real loser. Why does this always happen to me? Just my luck. Just like me to have this happen."

These statements lead to destructive feelings (in this case, feelings of self-doubt, fear, and self-directed anger). The person's subconscious mind, the repository of the self-image, is influenced most profoundly by emotions, and these feelings fortify the existing beliefs. In this way, beliefs become stronger, which is why our beliefs, once formed, tend to maintain themselves and why our behavior tends to be consistent.

The self-reinforcing nature of this cycle is shown in the diagram below:

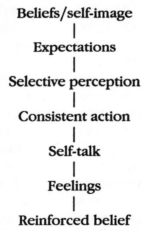

Beliefs/self-image
|
Expectations
|
Selective perception
|
Consistent action
|
Self-talk
|
Feelings
|
Reinforced belief

A person's beliefs lead to expectations about how he will do in given situations. As we have seen, he then perceives reality selectively so that it is consistent with those expectations. He then tends to behave "like him" which leads to self-talk and to emotions. The emotions, supported by the self talk, help to reinforce the belief as being correct, a very difficult cycle for him to break without help.

Limits on Success

In addition to limiting our perceptions and behavior, beliefs also tend to bind us to a given level of success. They tend to drive us to that level and not let us go beyond it. People who see themselves as destined for low-paid employment, for example, tend not to rise beyond that point. They neither prepare for nor apply for better jobs because it is not like them to hold such jobs. When confronted with opportunities to improve their skills, they make excuses. When thrust into a learning situation, they fail. Should they accidentally do better than average on one test, they will do worse than average on the next in order to return to the comfort of what is like them. By not creating an upward push toward excellence, they hold the whole organization back.

These instances are not due to any innate fault in the employee's make-up. The behavior results not from a lack of ability but from the limiting beliefs he has about himself. The beliefs were not present at birth but were learned by the employee as he became what is "like him."

On the other hand, a person who sees himself as destined for a middle-class existence, will tend to rise to that level and not go beyond it. If he finds himself in hard times, his sense of who he is will drive him to succeed—up to a point. But once his life is going according to his expectations, he will relax, avoiding any further progress. Both he and the low-paid person have reached a situation they are comfortable with. Both may envy people who are more successful. Both may wish for greater success. Both may resent the fact that they aren't as successful as others. But although they may be unhappy, they are not psychologically uncomfortable with their stations. They have reached the point that is "like them." And once they reach this point within an organization, they will have insufficient personal drive to push the organization toward greater success.

To explore how managers in The Winning Organization handle this problem, let's begin by looking at what we want in an ideal employee. If you ask a group of managers what qualities such a person would have, they will list qualities such as being a self-starter, taking initiative, being smart, being cooperative, being thorough, being able to see the big picture, being loyal, and so on. After they make such a list, the typical comment they make is "Gee, I wish I had just one person like this, but where can I find somebody with all these qualities?"

The answer is that the potential to be that way exists in every person they presently employ.

Development of the Self-image

When a child is born, he or she has all the potential in the world to be that ideal employee. The fact that so few actually grow up to behave in that way is in part due to the fact that something happens to them along the way—they learn that they are not the sort of person who exhibits the ideal characteristics.

On the child's first day in the cradle, no one could legitimately offer an opinion as to what the child will grow up to be like. Nonetheless, he is surrounded by people with very definite expectations of him. Many of these may be positive expectations, but too frequently they are limiting. Generally, people expect the child to grow up to be like his parents and like those who are in the culture surrounding him, exhibiting whatever characteristics and limits those people exhibit.

When the child is very young, when his brain is totally incapable of any intelligent weighing of what his potential is, he imprints who he is from the statements and actions and attitudes of those around him. If, for example, he is surrounded by adults who have very low expectations of themselves and of his parents, they will often have expectations that he will be like them. The child will tend to adopt these expectations about himself as part of his belief structure. If his parents consider themselves to be victims of forces beyond their control, the child is likely to imprint that he too is a victim, a person who will never get anywhere. If that child, in his childish enthusiasm, voices the opinion that someday he is going to be president of a corporation or of the country, the laughter of the adults teaches him that that isn't "like him." He thus begins to set up mental limits on his possibilities.

This sense of who he is is the most important thing a child learns. It forms his psychological gyroscope. It gives him a personality, a character, a consistency in his behavior. It develops and evolves in his subconscious mind without much logical input, long before he has the ability to explore what his true potential is.

As they develop, children also often imprint traits that go counter to the expectations of the surrounding adults. A parent who expects his children to be tidy, for example, may spank his child for making a mess, shouting to her that she is "a filthy little slob." The subconscious mind is profoundly influenced by emotional events and statements such as this, and it is also influenced easily by the statements of authority figures such as her father. After the spanking, she cries in her room, and she replays the traumatic event over and over. As she relives seeing the mess and feeling the spanking, the statement that she is a filthy little slob is recorded over and over and over again in her subconscious mind. From such experiences, the child may learn the opposite of what the parent wants her to learn; she learns that she is a sloppy person and that this is not a good thing.

Once such a belief is incorporated into the child's picture of herself, it is difficult and uncomfortable for her to behave in tidy ways. To be a tidy person wouldn't be like her, so even though she thinks it is not such a good thing to be a slob, even though she is unhappy with herself about this aspect of her character, she doesn't change her behavior. She won't behave differently in any consistent way until her belief about what is "like her" changes.

One of the paradoxes of all of this is that people can be unhappy and yet be uncomfortable trying to improve their situations. To behave differently than what is like them is alien, is uncomfortable, is stressful, and so they tend to return to the familiar, if unhappy, behaviors that they have always displayed.

When the child who believes she is untidy grows up and goes to work for the average supervisor, he may notice that her work is sloppy, and he may try to get her to change. In doing so, however, he is likely to fall into the same trap that her parents did and tell her that she is a sloppy person. This is not news to her; people have been telling her this for decades. All the supervisor does in telling her this is to reinforce her negative belief about herself and her possibilities. As stated previously, when he follows his natural instincts in such matters, he tends to make things worse. Although she may try to change her behavior to avoid being punished, she will not be consistent in doing careful work until she changes the picture of who she is.

Because we are hungriest to find out who we are when we know it least (when we are too young to have had a chance to develop much of our potential), and because beliefs tend to maintain themselves once formed, we all tend to carry around lots of beliefs which were formed by a very young brain which accepted the expectations of those around us without much critical challenge. This means that the people we supervise also are carrying around an image of who they are, much of which was formed by a two year old brain and which has little to do with their true potential.

Beliefs, however, do evolve. They can change and be altered in several ways. Supervisors can help their people achieve more of their potential by employing some of these methods. In The Winning Organization, with its emphasis on management as an enabler and an empowerer of employees, the supervisor is conscious of her effect on employees' self-concepts and so has a better chance to help them all develop the positive traits that both parties wished they had.

Affirmations

As alluded to in an earlier example, one way in which a person's beliefs about himself evolve is through the repetition of statements from an authority. The kind of statements that do this most effectively are statements that tell the person he has a certain quality. This is particularly effective when the person is a young child. A mother who, in frustration, repeatedly tells her child "You always wait until the last minute to do everything!" is likely to inculcate the belief in the child that he is indeed that kind of person. When this person becomes an employee in later life, his lack of initiative may stem from this early training.

Older people also respond to such statements, though not as readily. The employees we supervise will already have well-developed beliefs about who they are and will tend to resist statements about themselves that run counter to those beliefs. If the person wants to be different, however, if he doesn't value being a person who is sloppy, for example, or who never takes initiative, repeated statements from the supervisor will help him develop beliefs about himself that are more in tune with his own desires and which help him to achieve better results for his organization.

It is interesting that in our society, people are naturally adept at saying negative things that influence another person's self-image, but we are not used to saying positive statements of this kind. Whenever someone does a good job, we tend to say something about his behavior, not about his personal characteristics. "That was good work you did," or "You sure did a good job on this," are examples of this. But when someone does something wrong, we tend to talk about his personal characteristics, not his behavior—"How can you be so stupid," or "You are the most unreliable person I've ever met," for example. The former, while fine things to say, do not directly help a person develop stronger beliefs about his own personal qualities. A person who regards himself as a sloppy worker can regard his one-time, careful performance as a fluke. The latter category of statement does, however, directly affect the person's self-image. It tells him that there is something fundamentally wrong with his character.

Precision Management turns this natural tendency on its head. To get top performance from our people, we need to help them develop a sense of personal competence. We need to help them develop a self-image that drives them toward greater performance. As we will see in the next chapter, we also need to deal with negative behavior as behavior only, not as reflections of true character.

Statements that support a person's positive qualities are called affirmations. To be as effective as possible, these statements must follow certain rules:

    —They are present tense;
    —They are stated in positive terms;
    —They are specific, not vague or general;

—They focus on the end result or quality, not the
way in which it will be achieved or developed;
—They are honest;
—They talk about the person's qualities, NOT
about his behavior.

In addition, it is desirable, though not absolutely necessary, that
they have the following characteristics:
—They have an emotional impact on the employee;
—They are stated in simple language.

These last two are helpful, because we are trying to get our
message through to the subconscious mind. That is where the
beliefs about the self reside. While vast in its abilities, the
subconscious mind is not logical and rational like the conscious
mind. It responds most readily to emotion and is not good at in-
terpreting complex statements.

In order to clarify this concept, let's look at some examples.
Below are ten statements that a supervisor might make to an
employee. Which of these are likely to affect the employee's self-
image and which are not?

---

1. You always do excellent work.
2. You'll be our top producer if you keep it up.
3. It sure is nice to have you around.
4. This is excellent work you did.
5. I admire the way you always take initiative.
6. You get better at fixing this machinery every
   day.
7. You're too talented and capable to let one setback get you down.
8. I'm glad you're never late.
9. I'm surprised you had trouble on this because
   you are such a resourceful person.
10. You are the most careless person I've ever seen!

Now the answers:

1. If the employee does indeed do good work, this is a good,
affirmative statement. It tells the employee that he is a certain
type of person by using the phrase "you always." It thus helps the

person develop a positive belief about his behavior. This would not be a good statement to make, however, if it were patently false. The employee will know this is untrue and either think you don't know good work from bad or will wonder why you are lying to him.

2. This fails on the basis that it is future tense. It is a fine thing for a supervisor to say—it is good recognition—but it is not a self-concept enhancer. The person's belief structure can easily accept that he someday will be very productive without affecting the belief that right now it is like him to be lazy or slow. A person who believes he is a poor producer may tend to slack off in response to this statement in order to return to the safety and comfort of a world consistent with being "like him."

3. This fails because it is vague. It doesn't really say anything about what the person is like. Again, this is a fine thing for a supervisor to say. It is just not an example of the type of statement we are talking about here.

4. This also fails. It says something about the person's behavior, not about his character or what he is like. Again, this is good recognition, and it is the type of statement you should make often to your employees, but it doesn't directly support the person's self-image. As in example number two, the person may actually slack off in response to this statement if he subconsciously realizes he is doing better than he expects to do. He may indeed do worse than ever in order to average out to what he believes he is like, in order to avoid the stress of having his world-view challenged.

5. As in number one, this affirms positive qualities by using the words "you always."

6. This illustrates a way in which a supervisor can affirm positive qualities to a person in the present tense when the person is still far from his potential. A statement of the type "you are (the kind of person who is) getting better" is a present tense statement that doesn't cause us to be untruthful if the person does not usually behave in accordance with the quality.

7. This affirms that the person has the quality of being capable. It does indeed tell him what is like him.

8. This fails on the ground that it is stated in negative terms. As such, it gives the employee a negative image to handle, a picture of himself being late. It's like saying "Don't think of a green elephant." Suddenly, your mind is filled with pictures of green elephants. We want our people to have pictures of themselves behaving positively, so we need to change this to something like "I'm glad you're always on time."

9. This statement illustrates how we affirm positive qualities to a person when they don't do well. This will be discussed in more detail in the next chapter.

10. Although this is a terrible thing for a supervisor to say, it does indeed affect the person's self-image. It tells the employee that he is the type of person who is careless, and it is stated in dramatic terms which increase its chances of having an emotional impact on the employee. If he has strong, contrary beliefs, this statement might make him strive harder to show the supervisor that he is wrong, no doubt the behavior the supervisor wants to see. If he already believes this to be true about himself, however, his reaction will be quite different. His self talk will be "Yes. That's just like me all right. I am always careless." This cements the belief and hence the behavior. In such ways, traditional supervisors affect their employees in unthinking and negative ways all the time.

Affirmations and Behavior Modification

In emphasizing the affirmation of positive qualities, I do not want to imply that statements commending a person's behavior are of no value. Such statements are not only good recognition but may also help a person improve. Behavior modification techniques, where good work is praised and negative actions are corrected or ignored, can and do help employees grow and develop. Such methods provide the employee with much-needed recognition and encourage him to behave in more productive ways. Gradually, with repeated and praised successes, the employee's self-image, maturity, and self-confidence will also improve.

Precision Management

The use of affirmations, however, helps speed the process of behavior change. If an employee considers himself to be an average performer, above average work will make him subconsciously uncomfortable. He will be behaving in a way which is not like him, and this is stressful. To get back to his level of comfort, his psychological gyroscope will tend to lead him to perform in a below average manner the next time, so his behavior will all average out to be like him. Although the employee will be happy with the praise he receives for superior work, something in his subconscious will say "oh-oh; that's not like me; that was a fluke." Because the behavior is alien, it is uncomfortable, and there is a tendency to return to the familiarity of the old behavior.

Affirmations, then, are a tool to be used along with recognition of good behavior. They help an employee feel that the behavior was not just a fluke but is representative of his true qualities. It thus speeds the process of behavioral change.

Affirmations only work, however, if the quality being affirmed is valued by the employee. If the person puts a negative value on the quality being affirmed, he will resist the idea that it is like him. Affirmations thus work best when the employee has a negative perception of his capabilities and wishes that he were different. Most people with a "low self-image" have a negative view of themselves precisely because they do value the traits that they perceive themselves not to have. They thus respond well to affirmations from the supervisor.

To be effective, these statements must be repeated often. The problem is that the effectiveness of any one affirmation will wear out after the employee hears it a few times. For this reason, the supervisor needs more than one way of affirming a given quality to an employee.

Practice Developing Affirmations
Good affirmations often begin with words such as the following:
—You are. . .
—You're the kind of person who. . .
—You can. . .
—You do. . .

—You always . . .

Below are four, positive, personal characteristics we might like to see in our employees. For each, write five different affirmations which would help an employee strengthen those beliefs about himself.

—Being a self-starter.
—Being reliable.
—Being creative.

Try to develop your own answers before reading the examples below.

Possible affirmations for the first quality include the following:
—It sure is nice to see someone like you who takes the initiative on important projects.
—You sure are good at getting the ball rolling.
—What a go-getter!
—With a self-starter like you on our team, no one can stop us.
—You already have things done by the time I think of telling you to do them.

All of these speak about the person's personal qualities, not his individual behaviors. The second one, for example, talks about the kind of person he is, not that he got the ball rolling one time on a particular project. The person is being told not that he did one thing right—which he may or may not think is a fluke—but that he is the kind of person who does things right. This will give him a good and positive feeling about himself, and he will begin to look for opportunities to live up to that assessment. He will look for opportunities to keep that good feeling going by taking the initiative on some project. He can then be given recognition for that act and another of the affirmations above. Gradually, his belief that he is a self-starter will become stronger and stronger. This is one way, then in which we can help people achieve more of their full potential by helping them build strong self-beliefs.

Let's look at some other examples. Here are some possible affirmations for the second quality:
—I can always count on you.
—You are a marvelously dependable person.

Precision Management

> —I always feel confident when you have
> responsibility because you are so reliable.
> —You're as reliable as Big Ben.
> —I'm proud to have a dependable person like you
> on my team.

These statements are a bit more dramatic than the previous ones. If your personality is such that you feel comfortable making such statements, you may find this very effective. These dramatic statements are more likely to have an emotional impact, and so they are more likely to affect the subconscious mind.

Here are some statements that affirm the characteristic of creativity:

> —You always come up with creative ideas.
> —Whenever there's a new solution to be found,
> you will find it.
> —You're creativity is worth your weight in gold.
> —How'd we get so lucky as to have a creative
> person like you on our team?
> —I never cease to be amazed at how you can see
> situations in new ways.

Affirmations in the Face of Contrary Evidence

In the above examples, I have assumed that the statements reflect the basic truth in the supervisory situation. In the first one, for example, I assume that the person can indeed be counted on the majority of the time. To say that to a person who has never come through, who has never exhibited any reliable behavior would be a lie, and lies don't work, as was pointed out before. We therefore need to have some other ways of stating positive qualities for those who have not yet exhibited the desired behavior to any appreciable degree.

To dramatize this a bit, let's return to our example of the little girl who learned, perhaps to her parents' consternation, that she was a slob. Let's give her parents the benefit of the doubt and say that, with the one exception of their angrily telling her that she is a messy person from time to time, they do a good job of helping her develop much of her potential. She graduates from college at the head of her class, and, based on this, she gets a job with our organization. As her supervisor, you appreciate that she is bright, enthusiastic, and pleasant to be around. The problem is that she is also careless, disorganized, and sloppy in her work. Because her parents were clear that her sloppiness was a negative trait, she doesn't like being that way—it is a trait she considers to be a one of her weaknesses.

Before you read on, list some statements you might make as her supervisor which would help her develop a different belief about what is "like her."

The most direct way of doing this, of course, is to say things like "you are tidy", "you are neat", or "you are well organized." The problem is that she does not behave in these ways, and to tell her that would be a lie.

In such circumstances, one way to proceed is to look beyond the specific behavior to traits that include that behavior and other behaviors that she does possess. For example, if she is indeed pleasant and amiable with our customers, we can affirm to her that she presents a good professional image. By praising her professionalism, with statements such as "It makes me feel good to know you care so much about our professional image" or "You always do very professional work" or "Your professionalism helps our clients feel good about us" or "I'm glad you care what our clients think about us," we affirm a quality which does match some of her behaviors. We can also combine this with statements that reinforce her good behaviors, such as "I'm impressed with the way you handled Mrs. Jones. That was very professional of you." These statements, which recognize the behavior and do not say anything about her qualities as a person, can be followed up by an affirming statement such as the ones above.

When she hears the affirming statements, she will feel good. It is nice to have someone—particularly the boss—say something like this about you. She will then begin to scan her environment for ways to live up to this statement. She will—subconsciously—seek out opportunities to prove you are right. This may lead her to do more careful (hence more professional) work. The supervisor's job is to watch for this, to "catch her" doing something more carefully than before. Once we catch her doing this, we make an affirmation of this to her. We still can't truthfully say she is always careful, but we can affirm her improvement; we can honestly tell her that she is the kind of person who is getting more careful. Statements such as "Your work gets more careful every day" or "You are getting more organized all the time" are affirmations that will help her develop positive beliefs about herself.

One of the principle differences between a manager employing Precision Management methods and a traditional manager is that the former concentrates on "catching" her employees doing something right and rewarding them for it, while the latter spends her time catching them doing something wrong and reprimanding them. Given this difference, we shouldn't be surprised to find employees in the former circumstance being more motivated and ultimately more capable than those in traditional management environments.

Of course, affirming positive qualities to an employee doesn't work overnight. We have years of self-talk to overcome, and the person's social environment might be actively working against us. Affirmations are not magical incantations that produce immediate changes. Like everything else in Precision Management, this requires some getting used to, some practice, some persistence, and some perseverance. If the employee wants to develop these qualities, however, if he values them, we should see some lasting effects in his behavior in about a month.

Sometimes people object that this approach is somehow sneaky and manipulative. It feels to them that trying to affect someone's self-image is outside the proper scope of supervisory behavior. The fact of the matter is, however, that supervisors do affect their people's self-images every day. If it is proper to affect them without thinking—and often in negative ways—is it improper to affect them consciously and positively?

Moreover, as pointed out previously, these affirming statements only work if the person places a positive value on the quality, if he would like to possess that quality. As supervisors, we cannot manipulate a person into developing qualities he does not desire. A person who actively prizes unreliability, for example, will not become reliable against his will no matter how many times you affirm that quality to him. Affirmations work because the person wants them to. In the traditional organization, employees wish they had certain qualities and feel a lack of confidence because they do not possess them. In The Winning Organization, managers help employees make these wishes a reality. Effective managers use affirmations to help their people become what they want to be.

Affirmations are a very important tool for supervisors to have at their disposal. In addition to helping employees develop positive beliefs, they are invaluable in giving recognition to a person at level one on the control scale, as alluded to in the previous chapter. Without progress reports on such a person's work, we can give him regular recognition only in the form of affirmations, not praise for his particular behaviors. They are also invaluable in correcting employees' unacceptable behavior, as will be covered in the next chapter.

For purposes of helping employees achieve their potential, however, affirmations are only one tool and should be used in combination with other approaches.

Group Self-image

A second way of helping an employee develop a stronger self-image is through his identification with a group. If there is a strong sense of what it means to be a "member" of the organization, and if there is a strong set of positive values associated with that group, then the employee will tend to develop a belief that he has those strong qualities.

This phenomenon is easily seen in sports. Vince Lombardi, for example, managed to create a football dynasty out of a perennial loser at Green Bay by talking about the "greatness of the Packers." Even though he was referring to the greatness of the team several decades previously, his talk of "the winning tradition" and what it meant "to be a Packer" helped each team member develop a sense of personal strength by drawing on the strength of the organization's tradition.

One of the subtle reasons for the success of outstanding corporations is that these Winning Organizations have a strong sense of what is "like them." IBM employees, for example, draw extra strength from their identification with a corporate culture which stresses quality and service to the customer. Regardless of the personal beliefs-about-self an individual brings to the job, he develops the positive traits the group possesses by identifying strongly with it: "Of course I do a good job building these type-writers. I work for IBM."

This means that the manager who wants to build a truly outstanding organization needs to go beyond the important questions of "What are we trying to achieve?" and "How will we achieve it?" to the question of "Who are we?" What are the characteristics of our organization? What does it mean to be one of us? What kind of person is lucky enough to work here? These questions ought to be considered frequently by every manager, and the positive answers to these questions ought to be broadcast frequently to the employees to help create a strong sense of the group's standards and traits.

The means of communicating this information are various. In some Japanese companies, these beliefs are carried in corporate songs which are sung every morning. IBM, in the early days of its success, was sometimes ridiculed by outsiders for the slogans that were plastered on the walls, but these slogans contained beliefs that were adopted by the workers and helped to make the company the formidable competitor it is today. These common beliefs can be further communicated through management's internal memos, daily announcements, recognition of individual and group achievements, setting of priorities, and, as discussed in the next chapter, in handling unacceptable employee behavior.

One very powerful means of communicating "who we are" is the use of stories about the founders of the company or about particularly effective managers or employees of the past. These stories should demonstrate in a humorous or otherwise compelling way the values of the organization. In this regard, myths are just as effective as absolutely true stories. Just as Knute Rockne rallied Notre Dame by making up a myth about "the Gipper," so too can effective managers help their people feel pride and dedication to the values of the organization by telling stories that are only based on fact or even only on the spirit of the people involved. As one young executive once said to me of such myths in his company, "If they ain't true, they ought to be."

These beliefs about who we are constitute the "culture" of the organization. Culture comprises a series of values and beliefs that support its individual members' sense of "who I am" or of what is "like me." These values are carried in the silent self-talk and disseminated through the spoken words of the members of that culture.

The self-talk of an organization consists of the internal communication among its members. In addition to being communicated by management, then, an organization's cultural values are also communicated among the workers themselves. Effective managers are always on the lookout for instances of negative organizational self-talk, comments concerning the qualities of the organization and the people who work for it. Statements such as "This place is a joke," or "Typical management bullshit," or "Close enough for government work," (often heard in government settings) are danger signs that the common beliefs are driving employees to worse, not better performance. When confronted by this kind of evidence, managers should make a concerted effort to redress the situation, using the methods mentioned in the previous paragraph as well as holding meetings to discuss what it means to be a "member" of the organization.

This emphasis on the "culture" of the organization is descried by traditional managers as being "soft-headed" and "a bunch of baloney." "We're hard-nosed here," the president of a small company once told me. "I expect my workers to do what they're told, when they're told to do it, in the way they're told to do it. If they don't, I fire their ass." This person then went on to lament the poor quality of work he got from his people.

Managers in The Winning Organization realize that culture is extremely important. By putting an emphasis on creating a culture that carries with it positive beliefs about the capabilities and qualities of each member, the managers help each person come to believe that he possesses those abilities. If the worker believes, for example, that workers of his company do superior work, he will believe that, as one such worker, he produces superior work, and this belief will drive him to, in fact, produce superior work. Not to do so wouldn't be like him.

The culture of any organization is greatly influenced by its goals. This is particularly true of the superordinate, strategic goals that come from top management. Goals such as "provide the maximum service to clients," or "build the best automobiles," or "keep citizens safe in their homes," are goals which help give people a sense of what the organization stands for.

Many organizations mouth these goals without reaping much benefit in the culture, however, because the tactical results they are trying to produce are not formulated directly from these goals. The strategic goals become mere platitudes because the measurable targets the employees are pursuing have nothing to do with these goals. The employees thus come to think of the statements of top management as some kind of joke, and the culture suffers accordingly.

Upper-level managers frequently get frustrated when this happens. After all, didn't they announce that from now on, quality was to be the number one goal? But there is more to this than merely announcing the goal. As IBM showed when it turned around its typewriter assembly plant in Lexington, once quality is announced as a goal, it has to be translated through the tactical objectives of the company to everyone's job description. Assembly workers need to be measured on the basis of quality, for example, and rewarded accordingly.

Once the results and targets are directly derived from the superordinate principles, then a person can draw personal strength from those principles. "On our assembly line, we reduced warranty repairs by ten percent." This statement leads naturally to "We stand for quality at IBM." And that statement leads to "I produce quality products. I work for IBM, after all."

Counseling for Success

A third way to help an employee improve his self-image is to counsel him directly, helping him to visualize himself behaving more productively. One way to do this is to show the employee a list of the attributes of the ideal employee and to have him rate himself with respect to that list. Using questions such as "What areas do you think you need to improve in?" and "Which of these qualities do you wish you were more like?" you can help a person identify some of his limiting beliefs.

The next step is to challenge those beliefs. For example, if an employee says "I guess I need to be a little more reliable," we might ask him where he got the idea that he isn't reliable. Explain that while his behavior may not have always been such that it could be characterized as reliable, he has all the potential in the world to be reliable as anyone else. Explain that since he wants to be more reliable and has all the potential to be so, his unreliable behavior is in fact an aberration—it is not really like him. Explain that somewhere along the way he learned he was unreliable; his statement that he "needs to be a little more reliable" is evidence that he has a negative belief about himself that is unrelated to his true potential.

Explain to the employee how the beliefs reside in his expectations about how he will behave in a given situation and how they are reinforced in his self-talk. Encourage him to monitor his self-talk, to identify the self-talk that supports the limiting belief and to replace it with affirming statements such as "I am a reliable person." Encourage him also to picture acting in accordance with the desired new belief, to approach work situations with the expectation that he will do well rather than poorly.

This challenging of beliefs is also important if an employee argues with you when you give him an affirmation. If, for example, you say "You certainly are a conscientious worker," and the employee says "No I'm not," then you should challenge that: "Who told you that? Where did you get that idea? I guess you have been lead to believe this about yourself, but you've been tricked. It is obvious to me that you have all the potential in the world to be as conscientious as the next person."

Precision Management

Another way of counseling employees to visualize positive behavior is to have them role-play. If, for example, an employee needs to make a speech to a group, you could have him deliver this speech in front of a group of staff members. Instruct the staff to respond positively to the speech, to nod, to smile and so forth. Instruct them to applaud at the end if he does reasonably well. By creating a success experience for the employee (or several success experiences), you will help him imagine doing the thing well. This success experience can be followed by supporting, affirmative statements.

Similarly, having the employee develop highly detailed, specific, concrete plans for action helps him see himself behaving in a positive way. Before the above employee makes a speech, for example, you might ask him questions such as "What do you see? What does the room look like? How does the audience look? How are you feeling? What specifically will you say? How will you say it? What effect will it have?"

Employees are able to achieve only what they picture themselves being able to achieve. Helping them to see themselves behaving in outstanding ways is an essential first step in getting them to behave in outstanding ways.

Chapter 11

Positive Discipline

Managers in The Winning Organization take a fundamentally different approach to unacceptable employee behavior than managers in traditional organizations. The difference is founded on two principles we have covered already: managers must help employees meet their needs for growth and managers must help employees develop strong self-concepts.

Traditional reprimands, in which the employee is berated and threatened in an emotionally charged environment, never occur in The Winning Organization. One reason is that such an encounter belittles the employee, and effective managers recognize that their role is to empower their people; it is harder to get results from belittled people than from those who are empowered.

As we saw in the last chapter, the employee's image of himself tends to control the level of his performance. This image resides in the subconscious mind and is constantly evolving, though very slowly for most adults. It evolves in response to many situations, one of which is a circumstance in which an authority figure communicates with us in an emotionally charged environment. Traditional reprimands take place in such circumstances and therefore have a negative impact on an employee's self-concept. They are self-defeating because they lead to a negative self-image and hence to worse performance.

For example, imagine that a manager becomes exasperated with an employee's performance and shouts "Doggone it, James, can't you use your head for something besides a hatrack? You are the most dimwitted person I've ever seen. If you can't cut the mustard, you won't be around here very long." This tirade arouses emotions in James.   It communicates directly with his subconscious mind, the seat of his emotions and his self-image, where the logical faculties of the conscious mind have little sway. What pictures of himself does this statement arouse? It asks him to imagine himself as a dimwitted, unthinking person, and it conjures up the picture of being fired.

Reactions to Traditional Reprimands

How James responds to this depends on many complex factors, but the most important is his self-image when this reprimand occurs. Let's consider three possibilities.

First, if James has a strong sense that he is smart and capable, he may respond to this with "Oh no I'm not. I'll show you!" This is presumably the reaction the supervisor wants, and it can lead to improved performance.   It does so, however, at the cost of James's anxiety and stress, which may interfere with his job performance, lead to burnout, or lead him to try to escape the discomfort by finding another job in a different, better managed organization. It also breeds disloyalty and hatred for the boss.

The reprimand may also cause James to consider the possibility that he is not the smart, capable person he has always been sure he was. Although James may reject such a possibility, it does no good to dangle that in front of him.

On the other hand, if James's self-concept is that he isn't very capable, he will respond to such a reprimand by taking it to heart. Depressed, he walks off, his self-talk continuing the process the supervisor began. He tells himself that he is dumb, that he is a failure. He has been afraid that he wasn't cut out for success and this just proves that his worst fears are true. He imagines how awful it will be to be fired. He dwells on the unpleasant feelings of failure. He replays the reprimand over and over in his head. He pictures himself unemployed, desperate, helpless.

Because we get what we picture, not what we want, because we behave "like us" and because James now has an even more negative image of what is like him, his performance does not improve and may deteriorate. After more reprimands, more supervisory reinforcement that James is a loser, the picture James fearfully carries of his future becomes real. Rather than achieving results through James, the supervisor has achieved failure through James.

A third possibility is that James's self-concept is not either of these two. He doesn't see himself as particularly smart and capable, but neither does he see himself as particularly stupid and incapable either. From time to time in his life, he has swung back and forth around a center point. James thinks he is "average." In such a case, the supervisor's reprimand may tip the balance and push James toward the negative side of neutral. It may serve to modify his self-concept and help him develop a picture of himself as a failure rather than as average. In this case, James's conception of what is "like him" changes, and as his performance deteriorates in response to this, new reprimands accelerate the change.

In all three cases, then, the supervisor's reprimand, born though it may be out of honest, human frustration and a wish that James would act differently, produces negative results. Let us look, then, at how the Precision Management approach differs from standard practice. This approach, which is called Positive Discipline, contains ten steps, the first four of which are usually all that is needed.

Improving Performance and Self-image

The general idea is to improve work performance while simultaneously building the worker's sense of self-worth. In order to do this, we need to help the worker divorce his behavior from his sense of what is "like him." We need to focus our discussion on correcting the behavior, while bolstering the idea that he is a capable person. In this approach, we do not criticize the person at all. We leave the criticism to the employee, and we confine our criticism to his behavior, while making affirmations about his self-worth.

We then need to help the employee make a plan for improvement. Since we get what we picture ourselves being capable of attaining, not what we wish for, this plan must be very concrete and detailed—the employee must be able to see himself carrying out the plan.

Precision Management

This approach depends for its effectiveness on the manager having implemented the other aspects of Precision Management described in previous chapters, especially that of holding employees accountable for results. When someone is accountable and makes repeated mistakes, he will feel bad and be motivated to improve. What follows is a discussion of each of the steps of the process. A summary of the steps is on page 211.

Step One: Get them to describe the unacceptable behavior.

In implementing this approach, the manager must avoid getting into a stance of blaming the employee or of being his enemy. We want to act as a helper and an empowerer, not a belittler or an enforcer. If your stance is to help employees learn, they go on and improve. If you tell them they made a mistake, you are not telling them anything new, and all that will happen is that they will start to justify themselves and make excuses. In doing so, they may convince themselves of the rightness of their position and start to care less about improving. Our role in this process is therefore to help them succeed, to help them come up with their own plan for improvement.

As discussed in chapter six, we empower the employee to improve his own behavior through the use of questions. We want to say things like: "What have you done?" or "How would you describe your performance on this task?"

When you ask these questions, you are likely to get excuses as responses. Cut the employee off in such a circumstance. Tell him "I'm not asking why it happened. I just want you to tell me what happened. Just tell me what you did."

For example, let's imagine an employee who is often late to work. And let's imagine further that in this employee's work, lateness matters. (Managers in The Winning Organization care about results, not about numbers of hours put in, so punctuality in many jobs is of no concern so long as the results are achieved.) Let's assume, for example, that the person works as a team member and that his lateness means that others waste time waiting for him to arrive. Or that he is the receptionist and his failure to be there to answer the phone when the office opens has a negative effect on our professional image. We start out by asking him to describe the behavior. "John, I want to talk to you. How would you describe your contribution to the team here so far today?"

John says "Well, see, my alarm clock didn't go off and then my daughter asked me about using drugs and . . . "

"John . . . "

"And then my car wouldn't start, and the bus was late and . . . "

"John, I don't care about that. Just describe your performance so far today."

"Okay. So I'm late."

Before we go on to the next steps in the process, let's take another example. In the last chapter we discussed a character who was bright, pleasant, energetic, but sloppy. We have been using affirmative statements to try to get her to see herself differently, but today, again, she produces a report that is sloppy. We begin with "Shirley, how would you describe the quality of this report?"

She says "Well it's pretty good, I think. I was pleased with the way the analysis came out."

"Is this the very best work you can do?"

"Well, I don't know . . . "

"If you were to improve this, how would you go about it?"

"Well, maybe it could be longer, more detailed maybe."

"How would you describe the looks of the document."

"Oh, well, see, I spilled my coffee on my desk and I had to clean it up right away and the report was . . . "

"Shirley, I don't want to know why it looks this way. Just tell me your evaluation of it."

"Well, I guess it could be a little neater."

Sometimes, it is very difficult to get an employee to describe the behavior, and you will finally give up and do it for him. But if you can get him to do it instead, you will be in a better stance for the rest of the process, as we will see.

Step Two: Divorce the employee's behavior from his sense of self-worth.

Once the employee has described his own behavior, our job is to correct the behavior while simultaneously bolstering his self-concept. We do this by confining our discussion to the behavior itself and by letting his sense of personal worth "off the hook."

If the behavior is a rare occurrence we can say things like "That's not like you," or "I'm surprised." If John, for example, is only occasionally late, we can use this approach. This lets John freely discuss the behavior and how he will keep it from happening again without the need to be defensive about his sense of self-worth. John knows we aren't accusing him of being an irresponsible person; he knows we only want this behavior corrected.

On the other hand, if the behavior is a chronic problem, such a statement may be hard to make honestly. In such an instance we can still divorce the discussion of the behavior from the person's self-concept by saying something like "I'm confused by this behavior of yours. You're better than that."

Step Three: Affirm the positive qualities you desire.

Before we go on to dealing with how the employee will correct the behavior, we affirm the positive qualities we want the person to believe about himself. This plants us firmly on his side in the ensuing discussion and not only bolsters the person's self-concept but makes it easier for him to propose ways of correcting the behavior.

Let's go back now and pick up where we left off with John saying "Okay. So I'm late." He may be a little irritated about having to admit this, and he may also be preparing his defenses for the reprimand he feels is coming. But instead of criticizing him as a person, we say "John, that's not like you" or "John, I'm confused about this repeated lateness. You are a responsible person."

Or for Shirley, we might say "Shirley, you are better than this (not "you can do better than this" but "you are better than this"). You are a competent professional." Or "You care about the image we present to our clients." This feeds in to the program of affirming statements we began previously, as described in the last chapter.

Step Four: Get the employee to make a plan for improvement.

Now we have established with the employee that we consider this behavior to be an aberration, not an integral characteristic of the employee's personality, and the employee is disposed to want to correct it. We therefore ask questions such as "What should you have done instead?" or "What will you do the next time to make sure this doesn't happen again?" or "What can you do to fix it?"

As in step one, our primary mode is the question. The question empowers the employee to make the plan, it helps him own it and be responsible for it. If he fails to live up to it, only he is to blame, while if it is our plan he can blame his failure on the fact that the plan was unrealistic.

Make sure, at this stage, that the employee's plan is clear, specific, and that it can be visualized. He will not follow it unless he can picture himself doing it, so demand that he give you concrete details. John, for example, might say "I guess I could set my alarm clock earlier."

"That sounds like a good idea. What time will you set it for?"

"Seven o'clock."

"Is that really enough time to get you here by eight?"

"I think so."

"What time do you set it for now?"

"Ten after seven."

"How late were you today?"

"Twenty minutes. But see, it was cold last night, and there was frost on my windshield."

At this point, we are at a very critical point in the conversation. John is making an excuse here, subconsciously attempting to sidetrack the conversation from his not being on time to one about frost. The natural tendency at this point is to make an authoritative statement such as the following:

"John, let's be clear about your responsibilities. You are responsible for people who call here in the morning getting the information they need and for their regarding us as being competent and professional. When you aren't here, its hard for you to fulfill those responsibilities. If you can't fulfill your responsibilities, it means you can't do the job, and if you can't do your job, you can't work here."

Although such a statement embodies Precision Management ideas about responsibility and accountability, it is likely to make John defensive. It puts the manager in the role of the accuser and the demander. It tends to lead to more excuses, such as "Jack was even later than I was—why aren't you getting on his case?" Or it may lead to self-justifying statements such as "Everyone is late sometimes. You can't expect things to go smoothly every morning." In either case, we produce a "them vs. us" situation that makes it difficult to correct the behavior. Instead of starting an argument, we want to get John to be the source of his own criticism while we let him know that the problem is with this one behavior, not with his inherent qualities.

So we might try something like "John, on your way to work, knowing you were going to be late, what were you thinking?"

"What do you mean?"

"What was going through your mind about being late?"

"I knew I was going to be late."

"How were you feeling about that?"

"I don't know. I guess I was a little mad at myself."

"I thought so. That's the kind of reaction I'd expect from a responsible person like you. What were you thinking about how you could have prevented this from happening?"

"I was thinking it was just my luck to have frost on the windshield. I was wishing I had checked it out before I had read the sports page."

"Given that, what can you do tomorrow to make sure you can fulfill your responsibilities here?"

"I guess I should check."

"Okay. Now let's be clear about why I'm interested in talking about this. I want you to succeed here. I want you to achieve the results you are responsible for. You are a capable, bright, intelligent person. I want you to be part of this organization. In order to be part of the team, however, you have to be able to do your job, and doing the job, in your case, seems to require that you be here at eight o'clock. Now, it seems to me that your idea about checking on the frost on the windshield is a good idea. But what if something else goes wrong?"

"Like what?"

"You said it was 'just your luck' to have frost on your windshield. That seems to imply that other things like that sometimes happen that keep you from getting here on time."

"Yeah. Well, like yesterday, I couldn't find a parking place."

"You seem to have a plan for dealing with frost on the windshield. Is there something else you could do for the other things that happen?"

"I guess so."

"What would that be?"

"I don't know. I mean if there's no parking, there's no parking."

"And if there's frost there's frost. You have a plan to deal with frost. What about dealing with no parking?"

"I guess I could leave earlier so if I didn't get a space I'd still have time to get here."

"That might mean you'd be here early some days. How would you feel about that?"

"I don't know. I guess it would be better than being late."

"It would also give you time to have some coffee and get organized for the day. And you wouldn't have to waste all that energy getting on your own case all the way to work. Now that's two contingencies planned for. Are there any other things that you should take into account?"

"I don't know. I guess."

"Or are there any general rules you think might help you avoid this problem in the future."

"You want me to get up earlier?"

"It's up to you to decide that. The reason I'm talking to you about this is that I want you to succeed. I want to make sure your plan will work, that you've considered all the impediments to doing the job so you can fulfill your responsibilities. I want to make sure that you make the right decision because it hurts the organization when you aren't here at eight. You're too good to let us down that way."

"Okay. I guess I should maybe get up at a quarter to seven. That way I'd be able to deal with whatever happened. Boy, I hate getting up early."

"So do I, John. But I suspect you hate not being here on time even more."

"I guess."

"Now, let me also say that, although you are a capable person, I don't expect you to be perfect. Everybody makes mistakes now and then, and everyone has unexpected problems, even if they have allowed for contingencies. I haven't spoken to you about this before because you are a responsible person, and I expect you to behave responsibly. That's why I have been puzzled by your coming in late, and that's why I wanted you to tell me what you're going to do about it. When you are here, you do the great job you are capable of, and I hate to see that good work negated by this one problem. I'd like you to consider this a bit more, however. I'd like you to consider any other contingencies that you face from time to time that keep you from getting here on time. If there are some, I'd like you to see if there is something you could do, besides getting up at a quarter to seven, that would take care of these the same way as you have for frost on the windshield. I'd like to see your plan for all such things before you leave today. If you want my help figuring this out I'd be happy to go over it with you."

"You mean like with my car being hard to start?"

"Yes. How will you handle that and still do your job?"

"Well, I guess, since my car is hard to start in cold weather, maybe I ought to go try to start it before I read the sports page."

"Sounds like a smart idea to me."

As the employee describes his plan, you can, of course, disapprove any aspects of it you find unacceptable. If John's plan is that you will call him to make sure he is awake, for example, or that you should pick him up, you might well ask for a different idea. At the end, however, the plan must be the employee's own, not yours.

Step Five: Give praise for any improvement in performance.

If John is only five minutes late the next morning instead of his customary fifteen, or if Shirley's work is more careful than before, even though it is still sloppy, give them some encouragement. They are getting better. If all our people are constantly getting better, then our problems will constantly be fewer. Saying, "Darn it, John, you're late again," throws the improvement away.

So you say "John that is more like it. Now, tell me what you're going to do differently tomorrow so you will do even better."

This takes us back to step four. As performance continues to improve, say things like "You get better every day." Additional praise comes only for additional improvement, however.

Step Six: As performance improves, repeat step three. (See summary of steps, page 211)

Affirmations are particularly critical to build the employee's sense of being responsible, careful, or whatever other qualities we seek. Use the behavioral successes to underscore the fact that this behavior is "like him."

Step Seven: If behavior continues to be unacceptable, repeat steps one to five.

With most employees, this step, and those that follow, won't be necessary. Their sense of pride should be such that they are able to carry out their plans. There is always the possibility, however, that an employee's self-image is such that to straighten him out would be a lifetime reclamation project. In such circumstances, we need to begin laying the groundwork for possible dismissal, even as we continue to try to get better performance from them. Our posture in these remaining steps should still be that we are in their corner. We want them to succeed. However, the fact of the matter is that we are not running a welfare or make-work project for their benefit. We want them to be able to succeed in doing the job, but if they can't do the job, they should go find a job they can do. The principle should be "If you can't do the job, you can't work here."

As before, don't get involved in discussing excuses in this step. Concentrate on helping the employee develop a concrete plan for improvement. At this point, however, let the employee know you are going to document your concern. Ask for a written copy of his plan for improvement and submit it to your own supervisor. This lets the employee know you are very serious about this matter and that you insist on improvement.

If this succeeds in improving the employee's behavior, go to step five and six. If it does not, go to step eight.

Step Eight: If unacceptable behavior persists, give concentrated, one-to-one supervision.

Spend time with Shirley, for example, as she prepares her next report. Spot instances of carelessness or occasions where her behavior is leading to sloppy work and point these out to her. Indicate that you are doing this only because you want to see her succeed, not because you enjoy watching her every move. Indicate also that she is in jeopardy of being suspended if she cannot succeed even with your intense involvement.

At this stage, again reaffirm the qualities you want to see her display and give praise for even the smallest improvement. As you affirm these positive qualities, however, make sure the employee realizes that her behavior is still unacceptable. Saying "You are a responsible person," for example, is not the same as saying "You are behaving responsibly." Be clear that you demand improved performance if she is to continue to work for the organization.

Step Nine: If behavior continues to be unacceptable, suspend the employee in accordance with the organization's policy.

If the employee cannot or will not adhere to his own plan for improvement, and if the behavior is truly unacceptable, it is time to begin the termination process. The suspension is a warning that this process has started.

If you have been clear in the preceding steps, the employee will have no basis to object to this suspension. You will have documented your concerns, your performance expectations, and the employee's own plan for improvement. The only possible objection is for the employee to refer to your affirmations, saying something like "But you said you thought I was a responsible person." Should this happen, explain that you do indeed think he is a responsible person, but bring the conversations back to his unacceptable behavior and his failure to meet his plan. You might say something like "Although you do seem like a responsible person, the evidence is that you haven't behaved responsibly in this job." Ask the employee to think, while he is on suspension, about how he will live up to his ability when he returns. Indicate it will be his final chance.

At the end of the suspension, have a talk with the employee about his opinion of his prospects. Ask if he really wants to work here and if he believes he can do the job. If he gives an affirmative answer to these questions, ask why he thinks he will do any better this time. If there is a satisfactory answer to this question, bring him back at step eight status. Let him know, however, that if his behavior does not improve, you will have to terminate his employment.

As you implement this, again, focus only on the employee's behavior, and do so with reference to the results he is supposed to achieve. Refer to the minimum level of performance you will accept, and let him know that meeting that target is the definition of "being able to do the job." Again, if an employee can't do the job, he should work in another job.

Still, however, we should do all we can to help him succeed. Using affirmations, let him know you think he is the kind of person who has what it takes to succeed. Check frequently on his progress, and if he seems to be failing to meet the target, express your puzzlement as to how such a capable person could perform in this way. As before, he should have a plan for succeeding, for meeting the target, and again it should be his plan, not yours. It should again be in writing and should be submitted to your supervisor, your personnel office, or other appropriate authority.

If the employee improves but still falls below the minimum acceptable level of performance after all this time, you have a difficult decision to make. If you think there is hope, you can move back to step five. On the other hand, if you think it would be easier, cheaper, and better to hire a new person than to continue to try to help the employee improve, you may want to move to step ten.

Step Ten: If behavior fails to improve, terminate employment in accordance with the organization's policy.

The employee has been given every opportunity to succeed. With a lifetime to spend working with him, we might ultimately succeed, but the time has come to take the easier course. You have objective evidence that the employee cannot meet the minimum standards, that he can't do the job. And you have documented your concerns and his own plans for improvement, which he failed to carry out. It is therefore difficult for anyone to challenge this decision.

The manager's job is to get results through others, and one way she does this is by developing those others. Sometimes, however, it is easier and better to do it by replacing a person who can't do the job with one who can.

The Positive Discipline Approach is so powerful, however, that you will seldom have to resort to step ten. By reinforcing an employee's sense of self worth, concentrating only on his behavior, helping him come up with his own plan for success, and putting yourself in the role of trying to help him succeed, you create a climate in which the employee can grow toward his true potential.

SUMMARY: POSITIVE DISCIPLINE STEPS

1. Get the employee to describe the unacceptable behavior.

2. Divorce the employee's behavior from his sense of self-worth.

3. Affirm the positive qualities you desire.

4. Get the employee to make a plan for improvement.

5. Give praise for any improvement in performance.

6. As performance improves, repeat step three.

7. If behavior continues to be unacceptable, repeat steps one to five.

8. If unacceptable behavior persists, give concentrated, one-to-one supervision.

9. If behavior continues to be unacceptable, suspend the employee in accordance with the organization's policy.

10. If behavior fails to improve, terminate employment in accordance with the organization's policy.

Chapter 12

Looking Out The Window

Planning, which takes so much effort in traditional organizations, happens easily and naturally in The Winning Organization. In traditional organizations, planning is often conducted by a separate, high-level department that spends vast amounts of time, energy, and money creating documents that, in the final analysis, are often ignored by the people with line responsibilities.

This noncooperation comes from a negative view of the planning process, born of negative experiences. Many line workers have seldom seen anything good come out of planning. Their experience tends to be that anything truly valuable and creative has come not from the planning process but has "just happened." They find involvement in the planning process, if they have had any at all, to be tedious, boring, and nonproductive. And they find that plans either force them into nonproductive action or have no effect at all.

In The Winning Organization, employees' activities are linked, through a hierarchy of results, to an effective, strategic view of the organization and its environment. Even when there is no formal, written plan, the Precision Management process leads inevitably to a strategic orientation, an orientation in which the world is viewed from a variety of innovative perspectives with reference to what might be accomplished. The traditional perspective, by contrast, reveals the world only in light of what has gone on before. Having a strategic orientation is one of the reasons The Winning Organization easily outdistances its competitors.

Five key differences between Precision Management and standard management lead to this strategic advantage: the natural focus on the external world rather than the internal one; an accent on the future rather than on the past; a view of change as being the source of opportunity rather than of problems; the ability to act quickly rather than getting bogged down in deciding to act; and the emphasis on production rather than on processes. These differences, which are explored below, do not grow out of separate features of the approach but are interrelated, strategic benefits of the whole system.

Focus on the External World

One of the weaknesses of standard management practice is that it leads supervisors to spend a great deal of time thinking about the internal world of the organization, about the actions of people who work below them, often several levels below. Traditional managers are concerned with activities, procedures, and processes—with things that go on inside the organization. This often leads them to set goals with an internal rather than an external focus, goals such as "consolidate operations" or "move to new building," with the consequence that they lose their effectiveness in the outside world. It also leads them to meddle and tinker constantly with the cumbersome, process-oriented structure, spending vast amounts of frustrated energy struggling against the over-communication, political intrigue, and worker alienation that structure inevitably produces. In their concern with perpetuating standard procedures, traditional managers mistake opportunities in the outside world for problems.

By contrast, managers employing Precision Management methods spend a large part of their time thinking about the world outside the organization. They concentrate on the results they are trying to achieve in the outside world; they concentrate on the needs and problems of the customers, clients, or publics they serve. These needs and problems are regarded as opportunities by the results-centered organization: opportunities to profit in business; opportunities to serve the public in government; opportunities to solve community problems in nonprofit organizations. Being focussed on results in all their management practices, these managers are more naturally driven toward this outward perspective. They set goals that are externally focussed and phrased in terms of results to be achieved in the outside world. They therefore find it much easier to achieve success than their traditional, internally focussed counterparts.

This style of management was referred to metaphorically in chapter six as "looking out the window." It was posed as the goal for the manager, a symbol that she has developed her people to the point where she can give them degree of control number one and can concentrate her energies on the external environment, rather than on controlling her people. "Looking out the window," she finds it natural to think strategically, to focus on the environmental problems and opportunities her traditional counterpart is too bogged down to see. It is also a symbol that she is focussed on the results her organization is trying to achieve, that she has structured the work efficiently and has done a good job of providing her people with the motivation to do outstanding work.

Emphasis on the Future

This difference in focus leads to a different way of looking at the future and at change. Because of their internal focus, traditional organizations become committed to their procedures rather than to producing results, and changes in the outside world often make those procedures inefficient. Everything that comes along that makes it hard for them to do things the way they always have before is seen as a threat, as a problem to be solved. They constantly get bogged down in responding to crises because the world outside won't hold still—it is always changing, making it difficult to do things the way they've always been done. Just as management repairs one rent in the standard operating procedure, another problem arises, consuming more and more management time and more and more money, demanding greater and greater manpower. Eventually, there is no time, money, and energy left for doing what the organization is there to do, and it flashes out of existence in a furious blaze of useless, problem-solving activity—unless it is part of the government, in which case it merely reduces the services it provides and continues to limp along.

Management in these circumstances becomes an exercise in responding to "one darned thing after another." The emphasis is not on growth but on keeping things the same. Traditional managers adopt a defensive posture. Trying to keep things from getting worse, they desperately look for reasons not to try anything new. But the world never stays the same. The only certain thing is change.

The Desire for Change

In these increasingly turbulent times, organizations of all kinds are faced with an unprecedented challenge in dealing with change. Traditional managers find it increasingly difficult to be successful employing the old practices and the old priorities. They fear change and see only the problems it causes, while dreaming wistfully of a more certain past. As the present hurtles into the future, they become what they become in a series of haphazard reactions.

This defensive, problem-centered attitude of traditional managers leads to organizational decline—to rigidity, decay, and a loss of vigor. Energy is wasted on internal conflict and attempts to make the cumbersome organizational structure respond to ever-changing circumstances. Such organizations are lost in the fear of what the competition is up to and submerged in their creaking efforts to catch up. Traditional management, focussed on problems and on trying to keep people and procedures the same, discourages growth and gets stuck in the past.

Because Precision Management is an approach that is future-oriented, it is an approach that reduces the risks The Winning Organization takes in operating in a changing world. The manager using Precision Management methods is not confined by traditional ways of doing things; she is therefore better equipped to see the environment from alternative and innovative perspectives. She does not see things only in light of how they were done in the past but instead sees them as they might be in the future. She is better able to choose a future that is beneficial to the organization because she can generate alternative images of the future so as to have options from which to choose. Also, in "looking out the window," she is not taken by surprise by the events and developments that loom on the horizon.

This outward, future-oriented frame of reference, enables her to approach the changing world from a more productive perspective. Looking at change, managers in The Winning Organization see a different reality than traditional managers. They look forward to change as an opportunity to grow, to gain advantage, and to prosper. They see the present as brimming with opportunities while traditional managers see it as filled with problems.

This difference in perspective is a major reason for The Winning Organization's success and the failure of its less fortunate counterparts. The Winning Organization succeeds in part because its managers are never content with things as they are. If change doesn't happen to them, they make it happen themselves, creating their own opportunities. They are burning with a desire to improve, to be in the forefront, to lead their fields.

This attitude is the attitude of growth. It permeates The Winning Organization. It drives every member to increase his abilities. It drives the organization toward success in good times and bad.

The Ability to Act

The Winning Organization is also able to act more quickly and more effectively than those managed in the standard way. Traditional organizations bog themselves down in a profusion of standard operating procedures that destroy initiative and make change a problem. They bog themselves down in endless meetings to keep people informed, to give input, and to coordinate a fractured organizational structure. They bog themselves down because too many people and too many units have to be involved in order to achieve anything. They bog themselves down in the internal power struggles which inevitably arise as each frustrated, functional unit tries to gain more influence over the product. They bog themselves down in additional overhead for additional staff salaries, because Herculean efforts are necessary to coordinate all the fragmented responsibilities; these additional people often wind up creating work for others, leading to the hiring of more people who create more work to be done, a vicious circle of increasing numbers of internally focussed activities which are necessary only to make the structure function. And they bog themselves down in employee resentment and apathy because without a result to shoot for, no one has any sense of achievement; no one has the opportunity to win.

Process vs. Product Orientation

Traditional organizations are organized around processes, with the units of the organization devoted to functions such as planning, administration, quality control, purchasing, training, research, and so on. As we saw in chapter four, these units are often frustrated at having only partial responsibility for the organization's products and try to expand their influence over the product by enlarging their turf. The favorite target of such time-consuming, energy-wasting, turf-expansion efforts is a unit called "operations."

Organizational structures based on Precision Management principles are made up of product-based units. To the greatest extent possible the whole organization is "operations." Each unit has results to achieve, and each unit performs the various functions required to achieve those results. With their eyes clearly on the results to be achieved, managers in such circumstances are more naturally drawn to consider the strategic, environmental factors that affect the unit's ability to produce those results. They are therefore more likely to achieve such results in a changing environment than a traditionally structured unit.

The rule to remember is this: organizations get what they are organized to achieve. The traditional organization is organized around processes and gets a lot of procedures completed. The Winning Organization achieves results because jobs and objectives and plans are all based on what people are supposed to accomplish.

Strategic Planning Differences

This difference is particularly clear when it comes to the issue of strategic planning. Most traditional organizations don't do any strategic planning at all, preferring, perhaps, the excitement of being forever taken by surprise by what the future is becoming. Those that do strategic planning often do it in such a way as to make it a disruptive rather than productive activity, thereby forfeiting another advantage to The Winning Organization. Their planning is disruptive rather than productive because they do it the same way they go about their other functions, setting up a separate, process-based unit to carry out this activity.

Strategic planning units are charged with keeping an eye on the future and on the competition and with setting the broad goals and strategies necessary for the organization to succeed in that future. People in operations are then supposed to follow these broad directions. The activities of such a unit are indeed vital, but by setting up a separate unit to carry out these activities, traditional management forfeits many of the advantages of the strategic planning process. By placing the responsibility for doing the thinking in the hands of a group not engaged in carrying out the results of that thinking, traditional management sets up a macro version of the problems we discussed in chapter six—the division between thinking and doing leads to alienation of the doers. Further, since the people doing the thinking are not involved in the day-to-day realities encountered by the doers, the plan has a good chance of being irrelevant to those realities.

One way traditional management attempts to avoid the problems produced by the isolation of planning from the realities of operations, is requiring voluminous reports of the operations people. This breeds further resentment in the operations people, leads to reluctant and sometimes ineffective reporting, takes time away from doing the work, leads to hiring new people to do the reporting, and leads to an increasingly bureaucratic organizational structure. All of this reduces the organization's efficiency and effectiveness.

Further, the people who work in separate, strategic planning departments of large organizations often have had no experience in doing the work the organization does, nor do they have any regular contact with the people the organization is trying to serve. They tend instead to be people trained as experts in planning itself. Planners who worked in the boat-building company mentioned in chapter four, for example, had never had any experience building, selling, or maintaining a boat. The approaches such people come up with to handle future trends are frequently regarded as stupid by the people who are in contact with the day-to-day realities of the strategic environment, the people in the operations or sales or customer service divisions.

Strategic planners at a home-appliance manufacturer, for example, proposed to keep the company successful in the face of increasing energy prices through pursuit of a strategy of building smaller appliances with smaller motors. This plan was regarded as a disaster by people in sales, who knew that the customers of the company did not want smaller appliances, and by the people in the plants, who saw that better insulation or more efficient motors would be better ways to accomplish the same end. Nonetheless, the plan was followed, and the company lost market share.

Like all functionally based units, a separate department for strategic planning creates friction inside the organization. It leads to a "them against us" mentality and to conflict played out in the form of internal power struggles. Planning itself, as purchasing itself or word-processing itself, is not a very satisfying activity. It has meaning only if the plan is carried out and leads to a more effective organization. The planners therefore tend to try to control the operations people, to make them carry out the plan, and the operations people naturally resist being controlled in this way, especially by people with little experience in the work of the organization. Since strategic planning units tend to be found at headquarters, they tend to have more political clout than plant managers or sales managers who are stationed away from the seat of power. Planners therefore tend to win their battles and can lead the organization into ill-advised courses of action. Even when the planners are right, however, operations people may resist the right idea because it is not their own. This results in the organization's reluctantly doing the right thing instead of enthusiastically following an effective course.

In The Winning Organization, there is no separate planning unit. People with line responsibility are also responsible for planning, both strategic and tactical. Managers using Precision Management methods have the time to do their own planning because the responsibility for doing excellent work is in the hands of the workers rather than in the hands of the managers. Managers don't have to worry at night about the quality and rate of production because things are organized in such a way that the workers have something to win at work and are thinking about how to succeed. Managers also are naturally more able to do strategic thinking because of the outward, results-oriented focus of the Precision Management approach.

Further, managers have more time because much of the need for traditional planning itself is eliminated in The Winning Organization. Traditional managers spend much of their planning energies on solving the many problems that stem from the inefficiency of their organizational structure and their traditional way of managing. These problems, listed earlier in this chapter, are not solved by The Winning Organization: they are dissolved by the nature of the Precision Management process itself.

In The Winning Organization, managers concentrate on figuring out what the future is becoming and on defining the type of organization that will most likely be successful in that future. Precision Management gives managers the tools to make this desired future a reality. It gives them results-based goals that, when accomplished, will create that ideal future. And it gives them the Precision Management structures discussed earlier in this book, the organizational structures that provide those responsible for achieving the goals with the motivation and commitment necessary to succeed. Planning is the use of these tools to create the desired future rather than a process of responding to ever-changing events.

Precision Management Planning Advantages

Beyond the advantages of having been made by the people who will carry them out, plans in The Winning Organization have many other characteristics that make them more effective than those in traditional organizations. All of these advantages stem from the nature of the Precision Management process itself. As described in previous chapters, that process has the following basic features:

1. Management defines the "turf" of each worker, the thing the worker is in charge of.
2. With the involvement of the workers, management defines the results expected of each worker.
3. Workers are responsible and accountable for achieving those results, not management.
4. With the involvement of the worker, management defines how each person's performance will be measured.
5. Workers propose targets, based on those measures.
6. Management provides workers with the appropriate degree of authority to decide what activities are necessary to achieve those targets.
7. Unless the worker is at control level one, management checks regularly on worker progress toward achieving the agreed-upon targets.
8. The manager's role is to help the worker succeed and to grow in his abilities.

These basic features help managers avoid several common weaknesses of traditional plans. They lead to plans with vital differences in structure that give the organization a far greater chance of succeeding in the changing world.

As we have seen throughout this book, one vital difference lies in the way the goals are stated. The Winning Organization expresses its goals in terms of results. A bank manager, for example, might be given the goal of a ten percent increase in the number of deposits of more than $100,000. The problem-centered organization, if it does any planning at all, sets its goals in terms of activities—make at least three calls per month on prospective depositors of more than $100,000—and gets left behind by organizations that are less concerned with the activities of subordinates than with meeting the challenges and exploiting the opportunities of the environment.

A second advantage of the Precision Management approach to planning is that the plan vests responsibility for achieving each result in a person or a team. Many organizational plans set forth a variety of objectives to be accomplished by the organization in the coming period, but no one in particular is deemed responsible for achieving each one. When no one is responsible except, by default, the person at the top, we should not be surprised if the goals aren't met.

A third vital difference the Precision Management gives us is that people know how they will be measured in their attempts to achieve their goals. Without a means of knowing whether we are succeeding, there is no point in setting goals. Precision Management goals motivate employees because they give them the chance to achieve something, to "win." But if, as we pursue our objectives, we can't tell if we are winning or losing, there is still nothing to win: it is no different than having no goals at all. Traditional management, with its puzzling shyness about measuring performance, makes the whole planning process a futile exercise by failing to determine how employee progress will be measured and further failing to check to see if any progress is being made.

Yet another reason traditional plans often fail or are ignored is that the activities defined in the plan are inflexible. As a consequence, as circumstances change, traditional managers respond in one of two ineffective ways. They either ignore the environment and insist on following the plan to the letter, which leads them to expend energies in ways that are now less likely to be effective than when the plan was originally devised, or they throw the plan away and return to the excitement of "seat-of-the-pants" management, responding to each crisis as it comes. Such behavior may be preferable to the former, but it makes the planning process a waste of time in that the external environment almost never stays the same.

Precision Management plans help us avoid the problems of inflexibility in two ways. First, the emphasis on results leads managers to be more accepting of alternate means of achieving those results. The activities in the plan will not be religiously adhered to because they are not viewed as being as important or as interesting as the results to be achieved. Management is therefore not wedded to them and naturally looks for new ideas if the present methods aren't achieving the desired effects. Second, provision is made for reviewing and updating the relevance of the plan itself on a regular basis. Again, this is an advantage that grows naturally out of the Precision Management process. Because the plan is made by the people who carry it out, it is not viewed as a once-a-year project. It is viewed as a guide to success, as a means to an end, rather than an end in itself. It is a living, growing, creative tool made by the people who use it, for the benefit of the people who use it. As a result, the plan is more likely to be changed when circumstances require.

A fifth inherent advantage of Precision Management in the planning process is that it leads us to set time frames for accomplishing each objective. Traditional management often fails to establish any particular time frame for achieving goals, and in some cases never checks to see if the goals have been achieved. We should never be surprised if progress toward goals is slow or nonexistent when no time frame for completion is set. If managers don't regularly review progress, employees tend not to believe management is serious about achieving particular goals and tend to get bogged down in the details of the daily routine. Precision Management, with its emphasis on employee-set deadlines and on checkpoints for review of progress naturally avoids these problems.

A last, major advantage lies in the hierarchy of goals. Objectives pursued by each individual in The Winning Organization are more likely to be connected to a strategic vision than those in a traditional organization.

When the manager's focus is downward, the concern is with short-term accomplishments. By contrast, the Precision Management process, with its outward focus, connects the jobs of each member of the organization to the long-term, strategic plan and to the mission of the organization. Upper management pursues broad, general results connected to that mission. The next level of management pursues results whose achievement leads directly to those top goals, and so on. Such a hierarchy of results ties the objectives pursued by each member of the organization together into a unified whole so that the progress made by each employee contributes directly to fulfilling the mission of the organization.

A Case in Point

An example of the many planning advantages of the Precision Management process comes from a small fire department. This department employed full-time fire fighters at a central station and had outlying stations manned by volunteers. Paid fire fighters responded to all emergencies, and volunteers responded to emergencies in their geographic areas.

Before adopting a results orientation, management had been concerned with traditional statistics like numbers of fires, numbers of responses, numbers of volunteers, and hours of training. The growth in the district led to more fires and medical emergencies, and they felt good that they had at least twelve trained volunteers at each outlying station.

Once they began a more strategic examination of the service they provided to the citizens of the district, however, they changed their focus, starting with their overall mission statement. Previously, they had regarded the mission of the fire department to be one of responding to emergency calls, an activity-oriented definition. Changing to a results orientation, they defined their mission as keeping people safe from medical and fire emergencies. In examining the needs of the people of the district in light of this mission statement, they set a variety of goals related to prevention of emergencies. This in turn led them to become involved in a variety of prevention activities they had not engaged in before, activities that increased the value of their services to their citizens.

Another need they identified in light of the mission was for fast response to any emergency anywhere in the district. This in turn led them to evaluate the time it took to respond to emergencies in various parts of the district. The evaluation showed that in many cases, no volunteers responded to fires, leaving it to the paid fire fighters to respond. In some cases, this produced a lag of ten minutes or more between the time the call was received and the time fire fighters arrived at the scene.

Management of the district knew that a response time of more than five minutes could be too long in many emergencies. They therefore set the strategic goal of being able to respond to any emergency in the district within five minutes. Once that goal was set, all of their procedures could be reviewed in terms of how they affected the ability to meet this goal. Had they continued to operate without this strategic, results-oriented perspective, they might have never discovered they had a problem and gone on ineffectively operating according to their old procedures.

Three main obstacles to achieving their strategic goal were defined. The first was the fact that volunteers did not always respond to emergencies. The second was that old engines had difficulty going very fast up some of the hills near two of the out-lying stations. And the third was that some parts of the population could not be reached at any reasonable speed from any of the existing stations.

As indicated above, one of the advantages of the Precision Management approach is that major goals are translated, through a logical hierarchy of results, to responsibilities for individuals to fulfill. An easy way to insure this logical hierarchy is identify the obstacles that exist in the external environment (or sometimes within the organization) to the achievement of each result. Removing each obstacle then becomes a sub-result. In the case of the fire department, then, the removal of each of the three major obstacles became results for an individual or a team to achieve.

In analyzing the first obstacle, management discovered that while all stations appeared to have sufficient volunteers, in some areas none of these volunteers was available during the work day. From the point of view of an internal focus, there were plenty of volunteers; but from a results-based point of view, there were too few. Volunteer captains at each station, thus took on the responsibility for achieving the result: *Volunteers from the station will respond to each emergency in the area.* This led them to recruit volunteers who worked nights, were unemployed, or otherwise were available during normal working hours.

This one activity turned out not to be enough, however. As the Captains analyzed the situation in light of the result they were to achieve, they found that the volunteer fire fighters felt no sense of individual responsibility to respond to a given emergency. When an emergency occurred, all volunteers were alerted by a tone on a portable radio. Since there were seemingly "plenty of volunteers," the attitude of individuals was that if they didn't respond, some-one else would. As with paid personnel, we should never be sur-prised if volunteers act irresponsibly when they have no responsi-bility.

With the involvement of their volunteers, captains began to set up schedules for each block of each day and to fix responsibility for responding during those hours. Volunteer fire fighters were thus responsible for a result themselves: *Get the engine to all emergencies during your "shift."*

The ability of management to look out, to look beyond the con-cern with day-to-day procedures to the needs of the community they were there to serve, thus led to challenging results for the captains and the fire fighters. With these jobs defined in terms of results, the results were more likely to be achieved, and the workers were more likely to be enthusiastic, as explained in chapter two. This example, then, shows how the results of individuals are connected to the strategic plan of the organization when Precision Management principles are followed.

This same logical hierarchy of results applied in the cases of the other obstacles as well. To overcome the obstacle of no stations being located in some parts of the district, a citizen committee was formed, for example, and given responsibility to achieve the result: *Raise the money to build three new stations.* Committee members decided that the way to do this was to pass a bond issue, which they did. To overcome the obstacle of inadequate engines at some stations, an assistant chief took responsibility for the result: *Engines will have sufficient power to respond at maximum safe speed to emergencies in their geographic areas.* This led him to redeploy some existing equipment and to procure a more powerful engine for the district. It also led him to begin supervising the mechanic, whose new result, *Engines will perform at their maximum capacity,* was important to the assistant chief's achieving his goal.

Discussion of the Case

This example illustrates many advantages of Precision Management in the planning process. The plan is stated in terms of results, not activities, and those results are interrelated in a logical hierarchy. At the top of the hierarchy of objectives is the organization's mission. This is a broad, global statement of what the organization exists to accomplish, which is, of course, stated as a result. In the case of the fire department, the mission was to keep the citizens safe from fire and medical emergencies. A community action agency might say its mission is to develop the capacity of low-income people to escape poverty. A bank might define its mission as one of creating and maintaining an economically healthy environment in the service area. Or a city police department might say its mission is to keep the citizens of the community safe from crime.

Below the mission statement in the hierarchy are the broad results to be achieved by top management in the organization. These strategic goals are based on the needs of the population the organization is there to serve, the customers, clients, or citizens described in the mission statement. Needs related to the mission of the organization form the basis of effective goals. For example, based on an analysis of the needs of its client population, the community action agency might set goals such as reducing hunger, increasing employment of low-income people, and improving access to medical care. The bank might set goals of increasing loans to viable new businesses and increasing the number of commercial accounts. The police might set goals that included making the streets safe places to walk, increasing citizens' safety from crime in their homes, and reducing drunk-driver-related accidents. In the case of the fire department, we saw that one of those broad results top management pursued was that the department be able to respond to emergencies within five minutes.

Within these results, measurable targets are set by the managers, as described in chapter three. The achievement of upper management's results leads to the organization's making significant progress toward fulfilling its mission. In a similar way, mid-level managers are given results which, if achieved, will lead to the achievement of top management's results. Workers' activities are thus logically connected, through the hierarchy of results to the mission statement of the organization. In the fire department, for example, a member of the citizen committee who is making a poster to get out the vote on the bond issue can connect that activity to the result of getting money for new stations. Achievement of this result contributes to the achievement of the result of being able to respond in five minutes, which, in turn, contributes to fulfilling the mission of protecting citizens' lives and property. Every activity of every individual is thus focused on achieving the mission of the organization. Such organizations are more effective in making significant strides toward the achievement of the overall mission than traditional organizations.

Minimizing Communication Problems

This hierarchy of results also reduces communications problems. One of the most common complaints of workers in traditional organizations is that there is a lack of communication between upper management and the people who do the work. Workers feel that their ideas about how to do things are not heard or not valued by upper management. Further, they complain that they don't know why the organization is doing the things it is doing, that they don't know the big picture, and that they don't know the rationale behind the policies they are told to follow. They report that they feel unappreciated and ignored. "Top management doesn't know what we do" is a common complaint of workers in traditional organizations.

These problems are a direct consequence of the way the work is planned and organized. The long chains of command in traditional organizations distort communication, and much needed information is lost because it simply doesn't get passed along at all. Workers find themselves wondering why they are being told to do things a certain way. Their supervisors, who are also in the dark, do not improve worker enthusiasm when they are forced to respond "I don't know" or simply "because top management wants it done this way."

Because most workers want to do the best job they can, they get frustrated when they are told to do things that, from their perspective, may be ineffective. Lacking any knowledge of the rationale for the approach, they see only that the ability to be proud of their work is being taken away from them. When top managers detect such frustration with their directives, they misdiagnose the problem as one of workers not wanting to do the best job and traditionally respond by developing direct controls to try to make the workers perform effectively. These solutions to problems that don't exist cause further frustration.

In recent years, a tactic called "management by wandering around" has been hailed by many managers as the solution to the problem. They have found that they can close the communication gap by circumventing the chain of command, going to the workers and talking to them directly. In doing so, they discover much valuable information about worker perceptions and ideas and about the day-to-day work situation. They also discover worker misconceptions about their motives and plans and are able to correct these. Their interest in talking directly to workers also serves to make workers feel cared about and valued and provides some increased sense of belonging and recognition.

While "wandering around" does have many benefits, it also has its costs. The most obvious is that it takes time away from the outward, strategic concerns that ought to be top management's first priority. It is also very difficult to avoid undercutting the immediate supervisor's authority when talking directly to workers about their problems. And it is only a partial solution to a system-wide problem.

Managers in The Winning Organization do talk directly to workers. Their doors are always open to anyone at any level, and they take proactive steps to let workers know personally that they are appreciated. The primary purpose of wandering around—the gathering of information and the clarifying of motives—is unnecessary, however, because of the way the organization is structured and because the hierarchy of objectives dissolves common communications problems.

Precision Management

In The Winning Organization, managers are measured only on their progress toward achieving the results for which they are personally responsible. Because of the logical hierarchy or results, they will succeed in achieving those results if their people are successful. Top managers are therefore concerned only with the measurable progress of their subordinates toward the targets they set. These managers are, in turn, concerned only with the progress of their subordinates toward their targets.

Because of the logical hierarchy, where the achievement of lower results leads to the achievement of broader, higher results, top management doesn't have to meddle with the activities of those several levels below them. Workers do not get frustrated by upper management directives because they have the authority to determine their own courses of action to achieve their results. They do not get frustrated by sending recommendations into layer after layer of management sign-offs because their supervisors have the authority to approve recommendations related to the workers' results. Workers also do not feel cut off from the big picture because they can trace everything they do through the hierarchy of results to the mission statement of the agency.

In traditional organizations, decisions which affect each employee's work are made higher up in the organization. This practice produces planning and communication problems that are multiplied by the number of levels of management. Because The Winning Organization holds each employee accountable for achieving certain results, and because employees have the authority to make the decisions that affect those results, upper management is able to "look out the window" at the ever-changing environment. They use planning as a process of creating the future they desire, and they use Precision Management methods to make sure that the results necessary to creating that future are achieved. "Looking out the window," they use planning as the means by which the gap between what is becoming and what is desired is closed.

Notes

Notes

Notes

This book was set in ITC Garamond type

using ScenicWriter software.